Declutter & Manifest

A 52 WEEK WORKBOOK
TO CREATE
A HOME AND LIFE YOU LOVE

LAURA FORBES CARLIN

The author of this book does not dispense medical advice or prescribe the use of any technique as a form of treatment for physical, emotional, or medical problems without the advice of a physician or other healthcare or mental health professional, either directly or indirectly. The author's intent is to offer information of a general nature to help you in your quest for well-being. In the event you use any of the information in this book for yourself, the author and the publisher assume no responsibility or liability for your actions.

Published by Art of Everyday Living

To contact the author about speaking, workshops, or bulk orders of this book, visit inspiredeverydayliving.com.

ISBN: 978-0-9851178-7-0 (hardcover)
ISBN: 978-0-9851178-5-6 (paperback)
ISBN: 978-0-9851178-6-3 (ebook)

Contributor: Alison Forbes Van Hook
Editor: Shawn Mihalik
Book cover design: Abby Weintraub
Interior design: Shawn Mihalik

Printed in the United States of America

Declutter & Manifest

To my homes throughout the years—10514, 339, and 401—
for the magic, beauty, joy, love, and abundance you inspired and
co-created within your beautiful walls.

Introduction

Welcome! I am so excited to support you on your Decluttering and Manifesting Journey. I, along with my sister Alison, am the co-creator of Inspired Everyday Living, an online platform that teaches the transformative power of your home in creating the life you dream of.

For reasons we will explain throughout this workbook, your home can be the key to manifesting a life you love.

We have learned—both from our experience and our community's—that when you make changes to your home, your life shifts. If you wish to uplevel any area of your life—your relationships, finances, career—or if you would like to bring more love, joy, or peace into your life, you can support these goals by making simple changes in your home. Each week, this workbook will guide you in making small changes in your home that will have a big impact in your life.

Plus, working on yourself through the medium of your home is fun! We believe that using your home as a tool for transformation is one of the most enjoyable ways to access your best self and live your best life, because you get to create a home you love in the process!

Unlike other ways of working on ourselves, with our homes we have a chance to make physical changes that produce immediate, tangible results that we can see. An ordered, beautiful, clutter-free home, filled with the things we love, feels good! And these good feelings—this internal shift, not to mention the efficiency and empowerment we feel in an organized home—invariably ripples out to our experiences outside the home. Life starts to flow, and the things we desire unfold. A home transformation leads to a life transformation.

Alison and I realized this powerful connection between our homes and our lives early in life. We started decluttering and organizing when we were just six and nine years old. We thought it was fun to clean out our mother's closets and declutter and rearrange our bedrooms. This childhood hobby was also healing for us. During a challenging time when our parents were going through a divorce and we lost our grandparents in an accident, we found comfort in decluttering and organizing. Looking back, we realized that creating order in *our home* was a way to create more peace and calm inside *ourselves*.

This way of working on ourselves—of creating beauty, peace, and joy in our lives through the process of caring for our homes—continues to evolve.

Through the years, we learned that the process of decluttering and organizing has the potential to extend far beyond just creating a calm, orderly space that makes you feel good. We came to understand our homes can be the primary tool through which we access and support the realization of our deepest, most heartfelt desires. Simple changes in our homes support profound changes in our lives.

Alison and I have both utilized our homes to help us manifest many of the things we hold most dear—including relationships, children, and the special place we call home.

Of course, when we were little and cleaning out our mother's closets, we had no idea that our childhood fun would one day become our profession and calling! After experiencing firsthand the powerful role our homes play in creating our best lives, we were inspired to study with some of the best decluttering, space-clearing, Feng Shui, and spiritual teachers. This led to working with clients in their homes and a desire to share all that we've learned with others which, to date, has resulted in three books, numerous speaking engagements, several courses, and a growing online community.

This workbook is the result of all our very best practices, tips, and tools for how to manifest a life you love through the process of creating a home you love. We have seen how this process ignites positive change and moves our clients towards their goals. Let me explain why it works...

The "Manifestation Paradox": Why Your Home Is the Key to Manifesting Your Dreams

When you think about changing your life and pursuing your dreams, your mind might leap to all of the action steps you need to take, such as signing up for a course, reading books, and connecting with mentors, all of which can be very helpful. But there is an often-overlooked source of support all around you—your home!

Your home is a powerful tool for creating the life you desire.

Think about it for a moment: except for our relationships, our environments will have the greatest influence on how we think, feel, and act. And manifestations occur when you align your beliefs, thoughts, feelings, and actions with your desires. Our beliefs, thoughts, feelings, and actions determine our reality.

One of the most challenging aspects to successful manifestation is that you need to feel it, be it, do it, and believe it *before* it happens. We call this the "manifestation paradox." In other words, to manifest wealth, you need to feel prosperous before your finances improve. You need to believe you are worthy of financial prosperity and behave like someone who is financially successful. This can be extremely challenging if you are anxious about your finances and are far from achieving the abundance you seek. How do you imagine, much less embody, the life you dream of when you are not actually living that life? This is what is so powerful and exciting about working with your home. You can create an environment that supports you in living your dream.

Through your home, you can find ways to feel wealthy, live abundantly, and be grateful for the wealth you do have in your life. You can start living abundantly in a genuine and authentic way before you reach your financial goals. Your home can reflect abundance before the money is in the bank account. Something small, such as buying a single rose to place in a beautiful vase each week, or lighting a candle before bed, or placing artwork or photos that inspire feelings of wealth, or making a delicious meal, or setting the table using your best dishes and cloth napkins, can feel abundant!

In this work you are empowered to be your best self and live your dream independent of whether or not your goals are realized or your desires have manifested.

Simple changes in your home will focus your thoughts positively on your goals, inspire the feelings of your desires, bring subconscious beliefs to light, and support necessary action steps.

In fact, it is challenging to change without changing your environment. If your home is cluttered, disorganized, and does not reflect who you are, then it is likely you will not feel prosperous, much less uplifted, inspired, and focused. You will not be in a place to access or recognize the opportunities to move closer to your dreams. Also, if your environment is not conducive to the behavior required to realize your goals, it will be challenging to take action. Let's say your goal is to develop a healthy-eating habit, but your pantry is filled with junk food, or you don't have a place to sit down to eat because your kitchen table is piled with work, or the blender you need to create healthy smoothies is buried in the back of a cabinet beneath clutter. Trying to achieve that goal in that environment is like paddling upstream. How can we expect to change our eating habits without considering what's in our kitchen or how it's arranged? How can we expect to improve our sleep without taking a good look at our bedroom? How can we expect our lives to be different, or make different choices, if we wake up each day to a home that supports our old habits and patterns? We can't!

However, when you create a home that inspires the thoughts, feelings, and behavior that match and support your goals, you change direction—you shift downstream, moving closer to the life you envision.

Lasting and sustainable change—and the life you dream of—comes from changing your home-the heart of your everyday living.

Why Decluttering Is Essential to Manifesting

You may be familiar with the idea that, in order to get what you want, you first need to say no to what you don't want. Letting go of what no longer supports and reflects the life we want to live is what allows us to clarify and focus on our true desires. Otherwise, our time and energy are consumed by activities, tasks, people, and events that distract us from our purpose and goals. Similarly, our homes can be filled with too much stuff—stuff that ties us to old ideas, patterns, and beliefs—so much so that there is no room for new things to come into our lives! Clutter keeps you stuck in the past. Through the decluttering process, you say no to what you don't want and yes to what you do want. You make space for your dreams and free yourself to the present moment, where possibility and the power to manifest reside.

Here are the ways clutter blocks manifestations, and how decluttering accelerates manifesting:

Clutter muddles clarity. Clarifying your desires is the first step to manifesting. It is difficult to achieve clarity and focus when your environment is filled with meaningless stuff. You have probably had the experience of having so much to do, or so many things that interest you, that you became overwhelmed and ended up not moving anything forward. It is also easy to be distracted by the small stuff and never get to the most important tasks.

Decluttering promotes clarity and a positive focus. When you declutter, you keep only what is essential and relevant at this time in your life. By getting rid of the excess, you can place your attention on your most meaningful goals and desires.

Clutter takes up space. Sometimes, clutter literally takes up room in your home that keeps you from living your dream. Your dreams may require physical space; for example, your home may be too cluttered to create a yoga space to support your intention of starting a practice or to make a home office to support your intention of working independently.

Decluttering gives you the space to pursue your dreams. Once you declutter, you might be surprised to find that entire spaces, or even whole rooms, can be repurposed to better support your values and dreams. For example, a dining room can become a playroom, a rarely used nook can be transformed into a home office, etc.

Clutter blocks manifestations and stagnates energy. How can something new come into your life when your space is already filled to the brim? Clutter is a form of resistance. Clutter stagnates the energy in your home, delaying and blocking the good you desire from flowing into your life and delaying the experience and revealing of your manifestations. Even if you can't see the clutter—maybe it's tucked away in an attic or the back of the closet—it is still affecting you and taking up space energetically, blocking new ideas, inspiration, and opportunities.

Decluttering accelerates manifesting and frees up energy. You might have experienced, or know someone who has experienced, being really stuck in your life, feeling like nothing is moving forward. And then after decluttering or after moving to a new home, something really good happens, like getting a new job or a new relationship. This phenomena is a result of energy being unblocked. Something was let go and space was made for something new and better to come in. When you clear clutter, you uplift and circulate the energy in your home, allowing your home to become a source of positive energy and a magnet for the things you would like to manifest in your life.

Clutter drains your time and energy. Think how much time it takes to care for your possessions—purchasing, cleaning, repairing, learning how to use, picking up, and then getting rid of stuff. And this doesn't even take into account how clutter weighs on our minds!

Decluttering frees up our time and energy. Manifesting requires taking action towards our goals. When you clear clutter, you will recapture that time and energy, which will then be available to take those necessary action steps to realize your goals.

Clutter causes stress and overwhelm, and it can make you feel bad about yourself. Not being able to locate items and having a cluttered environment wear on our self-esteem. When our homes and lives are cluttered, we can feel like we are failing and can't keep up. Spending excessive time searching for things or feeling like our time is spent taking care of things—picking up, cleaning, managing- instead of living—can be self-defeating.

Decluttering is empowering and promotes a sense of well-being. Living clutter-free helps you feel more on top of things. You will be more efficient and productive, and you will experience a greater sense of calm and peace when you live in ordered surroundings. Anything that makes you feel better, that uplifts your spirits and promotes positive thoughts, puts you in a better place to attract and recognize the good things you desire.

Clutter keeps you from enjoying and loving the people, things, and experiences that matter most. Clutter is often a source of conflict with those we love. How many arguments have you had over stuff? Who will pick it up, clean it, repair it, etc. Our conversations and energy revolve around managing our stuff, instead of enjoying our lives and one another.

When you declutter, you get to experience more love and joy. When we are living in love and joy, we are a vibrational match for the good we desire.

Clutter reinforces limiting beliefs. Clutter reinforces limiting subconscious beliefs that may be blocking your desires from manifesting. When you hold on to things that are no longer loved and used (aka clutter) it is often because of a limiting belief such as *I am not safe, My needs will not be met, I don't deserve things I truly love,* etc. Beliefs rooted in lack, unworthiness, and limitation get in the way of manifestation.

Decluttering provides an opportunity to release and reframe limiting beliefs that may be in the way of you realizing your dreams. As you let go of the things that are anchoring lack and limitation, you affirm an abundant outlook and move yourself closer to the life you desire.

Decluttering will support you in clarifying your true desires, making space in your home (and mind) for your dreams to reveal themselves and focusing your attention on the things you love—the things in your home that support positive beliefs and your ideal vision for your life.

How to Use This Workbook

Each week, we introduce a concept and a corresponding action step or two. Some weeks are more involved than others, so it will be helpful to look ahead and plan accordingly. Also, please know that when it comes to the simple changes you can make to enhance your home, we offer many suggestions. Our intention is for you to have options, but don't feel you need to make every change. For the suggestions that resonate you will likely be inspired to take action. Some suggestions may speak to you down the road and some not at all. This is your home, and you will know which changes will support you in creating your ideal home and life. If the enhancement inspires love and joy, then it works!

The most important thing is to be consistent. Just keep moving through the weeks and taking action steps. Don't let perfectionism get in your way—doing something is better than nothing! You will see the steps you take and the small changes you make in your home compound overtime. You will create a home that reflects your dreams. And before you know it, you will be living them!

Ready to manifest a life you love through the process of creating a home you love?

Let's begin!

Week 1: The Connection Between Your Home and Your Life

"Every home tells a story. If you want to change your story, change the story your home is telling."
–Inspired Everyday Living

An intimate connection exists between your home and your life. Your home is a mirror that reflects your consciousness—and more specifically, your subconscious beliefs. Chances are you've already seen this reflection on display in your friends' or families' homes. It is always easier to see someone else's patterns than our own!

You can tell a lot about a person from their home. You have probably experienced visiting someone's home for the first time and noticing how much it revealed about that person. This insight seems to be particularly clear when you are dating and see your date's home for the first time. Think back to one of those moments. Do you remember what your first impressions were and how they may have played out in your relationship?

Write your reflections here:

Now let's turn to your own home.

Action Step: What Story Is Your Home Telling?

1. Find a comfortable place to sit with pen and workbook.

2. Take a moment to think about your home. Close your eyes and take a few deep breaths. When you open your eyes, imagine you've never been in your home before. Look around.

How do you feel? Write down any emotions that come up.

Which adjectives would you use to describe your home? Is it chaotic? Peaceful? Artistic? Cold? Lonely? Warm?

Write down some adjectives here:

Does a single person live here, a couple, a family? Does this person like to create and make things—or cook? Does this person meditate or practice yoga? Does this person work from home or outside the home?

Write your answers here:

What else can you see or feel?

3. Next look at any parts of your home you avoid or are your least favorite.

What feelings arise?

What adjectives would you use to describe these parts of your home?

4. Now ask yourself: Are these adjectives describing me, my life, a part of my life, or how I *feel* about my life or a part of my life?

And then, more importantly, ask yourself: Are they describing the person I want to be or the life I want to live?

Chances are that, through this exercise, you have seen the strong connection between your home and your life. This influence is why your home can be such an effective resource for changing your life.

Week 2: Change Your Home, Change Your Life

"We shape our buildings, thereafter they shape us."
–Winston Churchill

Your home is a powerful tool for manifestation. Not only does your home *reflect* your life, it also *shapes* your life. Your home reflects your subconscious beliefs, and it *influences* how you think, feel, and act.

You can see the influence our homes have on our thoughts, feelings, and actions both on a practical level and also on an energetic level.

On a practical level, if your home is cluttered and disorganized you might often feel frustrated and overwhelmed, or you may run late or procrastinate. You can imagine how feeling overwhelmed and stressed, or habits such as running late or procrastinating, will negatively influence your success in achieving any goal.

Think about times you felt that clutter or disorganization got in your way. Perhaps the clutter caused you to be late; get in an argument with a family member, your kids, or a roommate; or just made you feel really badly or stressed.

Write your reflections here:

Have you ever used your clutter as an excuse to not move forward with a goal or start a new habit or just do something you knew would be good for you?

Use these lines to write down anything that comes to mind about how clutter may lead you to procrastinate:

Here are some examples of how on a practical level your home will influence your behavior. Let's say you have a very specific goal to improve your sleep, and you want to adopt a habit to support that goal—such as staying off screens for an hour before bed. Yet your bedroom is home to a large television or has the charging station for your devices—or perhaps, doubles as your home office. If your environment is set up for electronics, it will be more challenging to adopt and maintain the habit of staying off screens before bed.

Perhaps your goal is to eat healthy and mindfully, yet your home "office" is the kitchen table. This arrangement may lead to mindlessly snacking and eating throughout the day.

List some habits you have been trying to adopt or a recent goal you have been wanting to achieve:

Is there anything in your home that gets in your way? List that here:

On an energetic level, clutter stagnates the energy in your home, blocking the things you desire from flowing into your life. Have you ever had the experience of something positive happening in your life as a result of decluttering? Or maybe you know someone who, after decluttering their home, started a new relationship or received unexpected money or got a new job?

Write down any examples of this phenomena that you might have experienced, read about, or know someone who has experienced here:

Also, on an energetic level you may find yourself subconsciously reflecting limiting beliefs in your home. A limiting belief is any recurring thought or long-held assumption about yourself or the world that blocks you in some way. We will go deeper into limiting beliefs in Week 17, but here is an example:

When I was single, every piece of art I had displayed in my apartment depicted a single woman—many of whom looked depressed. In my conscious mind, I desired a new relationship, but on the inside—subconsciously—I was feeling unworthy and alone. The artwork was a reflection of these subconscious beliefs.

Attempting to make a change in your life, embrace a new habit, or feel differently is challenging if you wake up each day to outdated or misaligned reflections (i.e., the artwork that was misaligned with my desire to be in a happy relationship.) Similarly, attempting to embrace a new habit is challenging if the visual cues in your home (such as the television in the bedroom) reinforce old habits. As Dr. Joe Dispenza says in his book *Breaking The Habit of Being Yourself,* "Your habitat becomes your habit."*

*Dispenza, Joe "Breaking the Habit of Being yourself." Hay House 2012. P.45.

You are much more likely to realize your dreams when your beliefs, thoughts, feelings, and actions align with, and support, your goals.

Throughout this workbook, I will give you tips for making simple changes in your home that will inspire feelings and thoughts in alignment with your desires and support you in releasing limiting beliefs and taking action steps towards your goals.

Chances are you already have a new awareness about the connection between your home and life. Now it is time to make changes in your outer world (your home) to support this inner shift. The exercise below will support your intention to change your life by signaling to your home that you are open to change.

Action Step: Kickstart Change! Move Nine Things

Move (and/ or remove) nine things in your home. You could move (or remove) more or less than nine things, but we suggest nine to give you a concrete start and end point. Also, the number nine is sacred in many earth wisdoms, such as Feng Shui, as well as in many religions.

This exercise is best done quickly—trust your instincts. You don't have to move large items such as a sofa or bed, but you certainly can if you are inspired to do so!

Here are some prompts to get you going:

- Perhaps there is something that you have always wanted to try moving to a different location? Go ahead! You can always change it back!
- Is there something that has always nagged at you in your home? Is it time to let it go? Or does it just need to be moved to a different place where it will enhance the space or be more functional?
- Are there items that you love stored in a cabinet or drawer that you could display?
- Could you rearrange, declutter, or curate framed photos or books?
- Could you group together a cherished collection on a shelf or tray to create a calmer, more ordered feel?
- Is there something that is no longer loved or useful that you can let go of?

- Could you move a very useful item to a more accessible location?
- Is there something you could move or rearrange to make a task easier?
- Is there artwork that you have been meaning to hang and haven't done so?

As you are making changes in your home, you are changing the energy in your space—and your life. You are signaling to your subconscious and home that you are open to new possibilities and reflecting your new perspective in your outer environment.

Week 3: Imagine Your Dream Home

"Imagination will often carry us to worlds that never were. But without it we go nowhere."

–Carl Sagan

Now that you have seen how your home mirrors your life, as well as how your home influences the successful realization of your goals, it makes sense to create a home that reflects your highest, most heartfelt vision for yourself. Your home should inspire how you would think, feel, and act if you were already living your dream. This concept gives new meaning to the idea of a "dream home." Throughout the weeks, your home home will become your own three-dimensional inspirational vision board for your life. Then you get to dwell in your dream!

Begin by imagining your dream home. Let yourself have everything you desire in this vision. Remember that this is *your* vision—be true to your values and who you are. Your home should reflect your authentic self, not your parents' or friends' or social media's vision.

Action Step: Imagine Your Dream Home

Use the prompts below to clarify what your ideal home looks and feels like.

1. Answer the following questions to get you started:

What does your ideal home look like?

____

____

____

What adjectives would you use to describe your ideal home?

How do you want to feel in your ideal home?

How would your ideal home serve your life and the lives of those around you?

What activities bring you joy? What kind of home would support these activities?

Are there certain colors, textures, shapes that come to mind?

If a certain style comes to mind, also think about the quality or value that is underneath the particular style (for example, underneath a traditional style may be a value of security or order; underneath a modern home may be peace and calm; bohemian style may be creativity or passion). If a certain size or location comes to mind, also include the values or qualities that are underneath these details (i.e. peace, safety, ease, creative expression, function, purpose, joy, connection).

2. Looking at the answers to your questions, what are five essential qualities of your ideal home? Write your five adjectives here:

3. Collect images in a digital folder or a Pinterest Board. You could also cut out pictures from a magazine or print online images and put them in a binder or on a vision board.

Week 4: Imagine Your Ideal Life

"Visualization helps us to channel the law of attraction, and to act from a perspective of abundance and optimism."

***– Dr. Tara Swart,* The Source**

Now it's time to clarify your intentions, goals, and dreams. The first step in manifesting, or realizing any goal, is to get clear about what it is you desire. Writing down your goals is the best way to achieve clarity.

Each year, Alison and I take time to make a list of intentions for all areas of our lives, such as Career, Relationships, Wealth, Health, Home & Lifestyle etc. We call these collective intentions a Life Design.

We spend a great deal of time on our Life Designs because they are part roadmap, part divination tool, and part stress reliever! This inner work can take a little time, but we encourage you to follow through!

Here are some reasons why it is worth taking the time to really dig deep and clarify your vision:

- Writing down your goals is associated with the successful realization of them. Studies have shown that when you write down your goals, you are more likely to be successful at achieving them. In fact, a study by Dr. Gail Matthews, a psychology professor at the Dominican University of California, showed that you are 42% more likely to achieve your goals by writing them down.*
- Writing intentions kickstarts the manifesting process because you have taken the unseen and intangible (your thoughts) and made them visible and physical on paper—you are already manifesting!

*https://www.dominican.edu/sites/default/files/2020-02/gailmatthews-harvard-goals-researchsummary.pdf

- Seeing your desires on paper creates space in your mind. Otherwise, we tend to recirculate these thoughts in our minds, which causes us to feel overwhelmed.
- Writing things down clarifies your goals and desires. You may think you know what you want, but when you put pen to paper (or fingers to keyboard), you may find you are less certain than you realized.
- Once on paper, you can see clearly what action steps need to be taken. For example, if your goal is to write a book, you can start committing to next steps, such as dedicating a few hours each day to writing.
- Once you have this blueprint for your life, you can relax and let go! You can trust these important desires won't be forgotten.
- When you put your heartfelt intentions "out there," your subconscious and the universe will start aligning and doing the work for you!
- Finally, in our experience, when you write something down—it happens! Not always in the timeframe you hoped for or in the exact way you imagined, but chances are, when you look back, you will feel that whatever unfolds was for your highest good. And sometimes the outcomes are even better than you could have imagined!

For all these reasons, we strongly encourage you to take the time to do this inner work and write clear, heartfelt intentions about your deepest desires. In just a moment we will share some questions to help you clarify your intentions...

You can see an abbreviated example of a life vision below. We encourage you to be as thorough and detailed as possible when creating your own Life Design.

Sample Life Design:

Values

- Optimal health and happiness
- Kindness
- Compassion
- Gratitude
- Love

- Peace
- Beauty
- Simplicity
- Abundance
- Grace
- Freedom
- Joy
- Wisdom and Clarity

Areas of Focus

- Relationship with Self & Purpose
- Health and Well-being
- Marriage, Partnership, or Romantic Relationship
- Family and Friendships
- Home & Lifestyle
- Finances
- Career
- Creative Expression

How I will feel when my dreams are manifested...

- I am living in love—feeling deep joy, profound peace, free, alive, on purpose, connected, healthy, and wealthy.

Intentions for Life Areas

Health and Well-Being

- I am enjoying vibrant and optimal health and wellbeing.
- I am easily embracing a daily exercise routine.
- I am enjoying deep and restorative sleep each night.

Finances

- I am gratefully and joyously celebrating financial freedom.
- I am blessed with peace and prosperity.
- I am well compensated for my creative contributions.
- I am making $_________ from my online business.

Home and Lifestyle

- I am feeling calm and joyful living in a clutter-free home filled. with the things I love.
- I am empowered and uplifted by streamlined, optimally functioning, and organized surroundings.
- I am tidying my home each day with ease and a grateful heart.

Career

- I am fulfilled and energized by a business that is serving others in creating clutter-free homes.
- I am celebrating the publication of my third book.
- I am grateful for the financial prosperity and success my work generates.

Marriage, Partnership, or Romantic Relationship

- I am experiencing deep love and enthusiasm with my partner.
- I am celebrating a relationship that supports me in being my best self and living my best life.

Family and Friendships

- I am a magnet for high vibration, joyful, loving friendships.
- I am enjoying love-filled, joyful relationships with my family.
- I am supported by highly skilled, loving, joyful people who support me on my journey...

Ongoing goals and habits

- Begin each day with meditation.
- Exercise five times per week.
- Drink water throughout the day.
- Before bed write down three things I am grateful for from the day.
- Tidy my home after breakfast...

Action Step: Clarify Your Intentions

Now it's your turn! Below are some questions to get you started.

Answering these questions will help you clarify your intentions and goals and what you would like to manifest.

Clarifying questions to ask yourself before setting your intentions:

Which areas of my life are working well for me?

Which areas are presenting challenges?

What are the things I value most?

Which areas of my life would I like to enhance in order of priority? (Examples: Finances, Health, Romantic Relationships, Family, Parenting, Friends, Career, Creativity, Self- development, Knowledge and Learning, Spirituality, Travel, Hobbies & Passions, Purpose, Home, Lifestyle)

What are my goals in the next few months?

1–2 year goals?

3–5 year goals?

5–10 year goals?

10+ year goals?

What are the top three things I would like to manifest (in order of priority)?

How would I feel if these three things were already manifest? What would change in my life?

If someone waved a magic wand and my life would be anything I wanted it to be, what would that life look like and how would I feel? Be specific.

Now start creating your Life Design!

Here are a few tips to keep in mind as you write your intentions:

1. Personal realm of believability: be open to magic and miracles AND be sure you create intentions that you can really get behind.

2. Write intentions in the present tense. For example: "I am deeply enjoying a new loving relationship," as opposed to, "I am looking forward to a new loving relationship."

3. Write in the affirmative. For example: "I am experiencing financial freedom," as opposed to, "I am not in debt." Also, begin with "I am" rather than "I want," otherwise, you will keep wanting.

4. Leave room for co-creation with the universe and for good that you may not currently imagine by ending with, "This or something greater for the highest good of all concerned in the most joyful and loving way."

Your Life Design:

Week 5: Energize Your Intentions (with the Help of Your Home)

"Intention is a funny thing, and whatever the brain puts its intention on is what it sees."

***–James R. Doty,* Into the Magic Shop**

Congratulations! You successfully clarified your desires and created a powerful vision for your ideal life. Now it's time to energize your written intentions with the help of your home by creating an intention table. An intention table is a place for your written intentions to "live." You can make an intention table by simply arranging loved and beautiful items on a table, shelf, or tray. You can then place your written intentions underneath or in one of the objects. Creating an intention table is an easy way to elevate your written intentions and imbue them with positive energy. Your intention table will uplift the energy in your home, inspire good feelings, and keep your thoughts positively focused on your goals.

Action Step: Make an Intention Table

1. Group beautiful and loved items on a table, shelf, or tray.

2. Place your Life Design (your collection of intentions) under or inside of one of the objects on your intention table. (For example, under a vase of flowers, or inside a book, or decorative box.)

3. Each time you walk by your intention table, you will appreciate the beautiful and loved objects. You will be uplifted, and the energy in this area of your home will be uplifted. From this heart-centered place, you can give thanks that your intention(s) are manifesting right here and now.

An intention table will support your manifestations in three ways:

- Changing the energy in your home; everything is made up of moving atoms. When you place any physical object in your space, it has its own vibration, and at the same time it is interacting with (and shifting) the energy in your space.
- Keeping your thoughts positively focused on your goal; each time you walk by, you will place your attention on your intention.
- Inspiring uplifted and aligned emotions; each time you pause to appreciate the loved and beautiful objects, you will get an emotional charge. You will start to feel whatever it is you desire—successful, wealthy, in love, etc.

Week 6: Make Space for Your Dreams

"The first step in crafting the life you want is to get rid of everything you don't."

— Joshua Becker

Now that you have clarified your vision for your ideal home and life—and you have created your own North Star in your home (aka your intention table)—it is time to let go of anything that is not in alignment with your heart's desires.

In order to manifest our desires, sometimes we first need to say no to what we *don't* want—we need to clear away the clutter. Decluttering creates space for the things we *do* want to flow into our lives. One of the best ways to make space for your dreams is to clear the clutter.

Decluttering is the number one change you can make in your home to change your life. And it's free! Decluttering is satisfying because you get to experience results right away. Even letting go of one item that is no longer serving you feels great!

Decluttering also presents a wonderful opportunity to take inventory of your life: where have I been, where am I now, and where would I like to go?

For the next several weeks, we are going to guide you through a process for how to clear clutter.

Let's begin with the why. Why clear clutter? In the introduction, we provided the many ways that clutter gets in the way of manifesting your desires and enjoying your ideal life.

Here is a quick recap:

- Clutter muddles clarity and your point of attraction by creating resistance.
- Clutter stagnates energy in your home, delaying and blocking the experience and revealing of your manifestations.
- Clutter keeps you stuck in the past or anticipating (an often negative) future. In either case, clutter prevents you from accessing the power and possibilities found in the present.

- Clutter drains time and energy that could be spent efficiently taking action steps to pursue your goals.
- Clutter causes stress and overwhelm and can make you feel badly about yourself.
- Clutter takes up space. Sometimes we need physical space to support our goals.
- Clutter is often a reflection of subconscious limiting beliefs that are in the way of you fulfilling your goals.
- Clutter keeps you from enjoying and loving the people, things, and experiences that matter most.

These effects of clutter are universal and hold true for almost everyone. Now it's time to take a look at why clearing clutter is important to *you*.

What Are Your Reasons for Decluttering?

Clarifying your personal why is important, because this clarity about how a clutter-free home will support you will help you stay motivated throughout the process.

Decluttering can take time, and there may be moments when you are overwhelmed and feel like it is all too much. Focusing on your intentions and your *why* will get you through it!

Your reasons for decluttering might be big values, such as desiring more joy and peace in your life, or it could be really concrete goals, like wanting to make a career change or improve your relationship. Or perhaps you wish to uplevel the little things that impact your day-to-day lifestyle, like finding more time to read, or practicing self-care, or enjoying sit-down family meals.

When you have a clear vision for a positive outcome in your home and life, coupled with a strong intention, you are more likely to succeed and the process is that much more powerful. So we definitely encourage you to take some time to think about *Why am I doing this? Why am I clearing my clutter?*

Action Step: Clarify Your Why

Here are a few questions you can ask yourself to get clear on *your* why.

How does clutter or disorganization get in your way?

Can you remember a time or times when clutter was a source of conflict with a loved one?

How much time do you think you waste looking for things? Is it daily, weekly, or monthly that you can't find things? Can you think of an example?

How much time do you spend daily, weekly, and monthly caring for your stuff (i.e., cleaning, picking up, organizing, maintaining)? How much time would you like to spend?

What are some ways that clutter and disorganization get in the way of living your ideal life?

How would you like to spend your time each day?

What do you want more of or less of in your life?

What brings you joy?

How would you feel if you were clutter free and organized?

How will a clutter-free home support you and the realization of your dreams?

List your top 3 reasons for creating a clutter-free home here:

Week 7: What Is Clutter?

"Have nothing in your house that you do not know to be useful, or believe to be beautiful."

–William Morris

What is Clutter?

If we are going to get rid of something, first we need to identify it...

Clutter is anything that is not loved or used.

Now, this may sound kind of obvious. And some clutter *is* obvious! For example, expired items, dried-up markers, outgrown clothes or toys, broken items...

And you may be thinking, *Of course I love the things in my home, I chose them,* but when you take a deeper look, you may find you are living with things that not only do you not love, but that also may be bringing your energy down and even making you feel bad about yourself.

Here are some common examples: Clothes that still have tags on them or that you don't like and will never wear—maybe you even feel guilty when you look at them. Or perhaps you still have an ex-partner' belongings in your home. Or a gift you don't like but feel obligated to keep. How do these items, these less obvious kinds of clutter, make you feel? Chances are, not loved or in love.

And we really want to aim for love—we can choose love in our homes!

If you are surrounding yourself with things that are not loved—and are not in alignment with your ideal vision, your values, or your heartfelt dreams you ask yourself, why? Why am I settling for less than love?

If you wish to live your unique version of your ideal life, then don't settle for things that are less than a reflection of your ideals. Instead, surround yourself with things that support your goals and reflect your ideals- things that inspire you, feed you, lift you up, make your heart sing, and bring you joy!

The things we don't love—this less obvious kind of clutter—can be the most challenging to let go of *and* can typically have the greatest impact on our life. We will revisit this more challenging type of clutter down the road and give you tips for how to handle it. For now, let's get the energy moving in your home and life by decluttering some of the more obvious types of clutter. These easy wins will free up energy, make you feel better, and motivate you and prepare you for the more challenging areas.

I will be outlining a more thorough decluttering process in the next weeks, but we figured by now you might be excited to get started! The action step below will help you start making space, and you will see how good it feels to let go of even one item or clear one drawer—and how much you can get done in a small amount of time!

Action Step: Declutter the "Obvious" Types of Clutter

Grab a box or bag and set a timer for 15-30 minutes. Place any items that are no longer loved or used in the box or bag and discard them appropriately (i.e., recycle or trash).

Tips to start:

- Begin with easy-to-let-go-of items such as expired food, dried-up pens and markers, Tupperware with missing lids, empty shampoo bottles, dried-up makeup, stained items or items in disrepair that cannot be fixed, old magazines, outdated cords or chargers, parts that don't belong to anything, manuals or warranties for items you no longer own, extra plastic or paper grocery bags, etc.
- Choose a very small area that can be decluttered in 15-30 minutes such as your wallet or purse, gym bag, baby bag, car, medicine cabinet, refrigerator, not-too-cluttered drawer, cabinet or shelf, junk drawer, coffee table, bedside table etc.
- See the appendix for a list of "obvious," typically easy-to-let-go-of, clutter.

Week 8: Support Your Decluttering, Part I

"If you have the courage to start, you have the courage to succeed."

–Mel Robbins

Last week, you started to create space in your home by spending 15 to 30 minutes clearing clutter. You might have been surprised by how much clutter you were able to let go of in this short amount of time. And you also probably experienced how good it feels to clear and how easy it can be with just a timer and a box. If this exercise works for you—keep going! You can even make it a daily habit. A little bit everyday adds up! Even if you removed just one piece of clutter from your home everyday, that would be 365 fewer items over these 52 weeks!

Sometimes this "something is better than nothing" approach is the way to go, particularly if you do not have room in your calendar to set aside large blocks of time devoted to decluttering. However, sometimes it helps to have a plan and a process. A little preparation on the front end can set you up for success and make the process more efficient and save time in the long run.

The first thing you can do to prepare is create a clutter-clearing plan. It is very common to have inner clutter about our physical clutter! Just thinking about our physical clutter can be overwhelming. One of the best ways to support your decluttering and to feel less overwhelmed is to make a clutter-clearing plan.

A clutter-clearing plan is a simple checklist of the rooms in your home broken down into areas, and it will clear your inner clutter about clutter! You will feel less overwhelmed, because you will see that there is a beginning and endpoint to your decluttering. You will have a roadmap that will guide you into action and a checklist to keep you motivated.

The clutter-clearing plan will also help you break down your decluttering into manageable tasks that work with your schedule and available time.

It is a common misconception that decluttering needs to happen all at once—and that you need to take apart your entire kitchen in order to declutter. Not only is this too overwhelming for some people, but you may not have that kind of time. You may only have twenty minutes a day or a few hours on the weekend. The clutter-clearing plan will support you in decluttering in small chunks of time and keep you on track for eventually addressing each and every item in your home.

Remember: it is better to do something rather than nothing! The longer you wait, the longer you delay your dreams and the joy of living in a clutter-free space.

The important thing is to commit. Either schedule blocks of time in your calendar to declutter (2–4 hours is ideal), or if you need to go little by little, choose where in your daily routine you will incorporate 15–30 minutes of decluttering—for example, after making beds and tidying up in the morning, or after lunch.

Action Step: Make a Clutter-Clearing Plan

1. Make a list of all the rooms in your home. You can use the template in Appendix 2 and customize it to fit your home and schedule.

2. Under each room, write down the areas of the room that need to be decluttered. Under "living room," you may write coffee table, TV cabinet, and bookshelves. Under "primary bedroom," you may write bedside table, closet, and armoire.

3. Depending on the increments of time you have to declutter, you may wish to break the list down further. "Closet" could be broken down into types of clothes such as tops, bottoms, shoes, coats and jackets, etc. Books could be broken down into cookbooks, coffee table books, resources, non-fiction, fiction, etc.

Be sure to check off each area as you complete it! Our brains are satisfied and motivated by completion!

P.S. If you need inspiration for your clutter-clearing plan, you can check out the list of areas to declutter in the back of this journal.

Week 9: Support Your Decluttering, Part 2

"Before anything else, preparation is the key to success."
–Alexander Graham Bell

Another way to support your decluttering is to have bags and boxes ready for the items you choose to give away. You will see that decluttering is a lot easier if you keep moving.

Not knowing where to put something you have chosen to give away, or not having certain helpful tools on hand, can derail your efforts. So it's helpful to put together a declutter "tool-kit" before you begin!

Action Step: Plan Ahead For Give-Aways

Gather and label the following items:

- Trash bag
- Recycle bag
- Donations box
- Sell box
- To-do box (i.e., things that may need a repair or battery)
- Relocate (things that belong in a different part of the house)

You may also want to have on hand:

- A dust rag and cleaning products.
- Post-it notes, or small pieces of paper and tape, so you can write down what action step is required for the item and post or tape it to the item. This way, when you revisit the action-step bin, you don't have to remember.
- Consider having some empty clear plastic bins with lids on hand

for projects you may come across as you declutter. Label the bins with details about the project (i.e., photos that need to be scanned or put into albums, or videos that need to be uploaded)

Plan ahead for donating, selling, or disposing (i.e., decide where you will donate; if you plan to sell on eBay, set up an account; etc.).

Be realistic: if you are overwhelmed by clutter, any donation center will do! Also consider whether or not it is worth your time to sell! Down the road, when you are more clutter-free, you can refine how and where you donate.

Week 10: Three-Step Declutter

"The ability to simplify means to eliminate the unnecessary so that the necessary may speak."

–Hans Hofmann

Now that you have your declutter toolkit ready to go, it's time to start clearing using our simple 3-step process!

1. Take everything out: Empty the drawer, remove things off the shelf, take everything out of the closet, and place the items on the floor, a table, or bed. This step is so important, because it is the only way to ensure you address each and every item. Otherwise, it is too easy to "cheat" and gloss over or avoid certain items.

2. Clean: Physically clean the space before putting anything back. When you have a freshly cleaned, empty space, you will be so much more mindful about what you choose to put back.

3. Determine whether the item is loved and or used: This is the heart of the process! Engage with each item. Touch it or hold it. Ask yourself whether the item is loved or used?

For useful items, ask questions such as: When is the last time I used it? Do I have multiples? Could I do without?

For items that are more sentimental or decorative, you will observe your thoughts, your feelings, and especially your body. If right away the item elicits negative memories or emotions, then chances are the item is no longer loved. Tune into your body. Invariably, when we love something, we feel uplifted and breathe more deeply. When something is not loved, it tends to create a tugging or nagging feeling.

Items you choose to keep can go back where they came from (unless you know they belong in a different place, in which case they can go into the "relocate" bin.) When you put the items back, you can think of this as "temporary" storage, as we will explain in just a moment. Place items you choose to let go of in the appropriate box or bag (i.e., trash, recycle, donate, or sell.)

There are three guidelines to keep in mind while you clear:

1. Finish decluttering before you start organizing. The biggest decluttering mistake is to try to organize before you finish decluttering. You simply can't organize clutter! You will waste time and energy trying. Also, you will waste money, because you may think you need all kinds of organizing items such as baskets, bins, drawer dividers, etc. But often after you declutter, little to no organization is required. A clutter-free drawer is inherently organized. Yet another reason to declutter first is that there is a domino effect when you declutter—you will likely create space in drawers, closets, shelves, cabinets—and sometimes in entire rooms. This new space will change your home's storage capacity and will lead to storing things in locations you will not know you have until the decluttering process is complete.

2. Cull like items. If you are decluttering your clothes in the master bedroom, bring any clothes you have stored in other areas of your house into your bedroom so you can address all your clothes at once. If you are decluttering your living room and also keep books in your office and bedside table, then bring the books to the living room. Conversely, if you are decluttering the family room and your child's toys are in this room, you can put those back in their bedroom or playroom and address them when you get to those rooms.

3. Commit to your entire home. If you wish to reach a new level of simplicity and never have this amount of clutter again, you need to address every item in your home. The clutter-clearing plan allows you to start small, go room by room, and still be on track to complete your entire home, whether that takes days, weeks, months, or a year. We suggest going room by room and completing one room before you move on to the next. Knowing you have completed a room on your plan will give you the experience of living clutter free in that room. This will inspire you to keep going!

Action Step: Choose an Area

Choose an area on your cluttering-clearing plan. We suggest starting with an easy—meaning not-too-cluttered—area, because completion of an easy area will motivate you for the more challenging areas.

Use the three-step declutter process and start clearing

Remember to check the box when you are done, and then move on to the next area!

Week II: Tips for Decluttering

"Simplicity boils down to two things: Identify the essential, and eliminate the rest."

–Leo Babauta

The more you declutter, the easier and more enjoyable it can be. Many people find the process similar to a meditation—we call this decluttering flow. Below are a few helpful tips to keep in mind as you declutter and help you find your decluttering flow.

Photograph: If you find it difficult to let go of an item, try taking a photo! Knowing you have the photograph makes it easier to let go of the item, particularly if it is a sentimental item. And it saves physical space in your home. We find this particularly helpful for letters and birthday cards and other memorabilia. You can always include these photos in a yearly album, where you will be more apt to reread and enjoy the sentiments.

Scan: Scanning documents that don't require you to keep the original saves space. Just make sure you have a system of organized digital folders, or you will end up with digital clutter—I know firsthand as this is my clutter weak spot.

Keep a wish list: Sometimes when we declutter, we think of all the things we "need" or wish to buy. If you find yourself thinking of items you wish to purchase, then write the item down on a wish list and wait for 30 days. Chances are, when you look back on this list 30 days from now, you won't even remember why you felt you needed it in the first place.

Keep moving: There is no need to over-deliberate while you declutter. If you can't decide whether or not to let go of an item, just go ahead and keep it. Decluttering is a heart-centered process. If we over-deliberate or start thinking about where we will house things (aka organizing), we can get stuck in our heads. If you come across a task, such as a toy that needs a battery, place it in your "to do" basket. When addressing photos, go ahead and choose the ones that are loved and useful, but refrain from putting them in albums (that would be organizing.) Just place them in a container labeled "photos to be put into albums." The more you keep moving, the more you will find your decluttering flow.

Curate Collections: If you find you no longer love your collection, or could do with less, you can photograph the collection or choose to keep one (of the smaller items) in the collection.

Action step: Keep Decluttering!

As we said in Week 8, decide whether you will build clutter-clearing into your daily routine, (i.e., after breakfast, after dropping kids at school...) or will schedule time to clear. If you schedule time, make sure you put it in your calendar like any other important event!

Where in my daily routine will I commit to 15–30 minutes to decluttering?

- [ ] I have scheduled decluttering time in my calendar.

Week 12: How to Let Go of Clutter

"If you want to feel light, you have to let go."
–Courtney Carver

At this point, you have likely filled some of your bags and boxes. Now it is time to get these items out of the house. Have you ever found yourself hesitating to get your giveaway items out the door? You may even have the inclination to rifle through the boxes again (which is not advised!).

Gratitude and intention will make it easier to let go.

Gratitude

Marie Kondo, the world-renowned organizing expert and author of *The Life Changing Magic Of Tidying Up*, provides us with a wonderful way to let go of the things in our lives that are no longer loved or useful: thanking your items out loud. You can be grateful for how they served you, grateful for the person who gave them to you, or grateful that you had the prosperity in your life to afford all of this stuff. You can also be grateful to these items for showing you what no longer works in your life.

When you choose to let go of an item, thank the item for serving you and then place it in your donate or sell pile. Or, once your bags and boxes are ready to be donated, give a collective thank you to all the items.

Expressing gratitude moves us out of our heads—where we may be judging ourselves for having wasted money or accumulated clutter—and into our hearts.

Sometimes we hold on because we are worried our needs won't be met. We settle for things we don't love and items that do not reflect our ideals because we are afraid we are not deserving of more. Letting go of these types of items is an act of self-love and trust. You are affirming to yourself that you are worthy of love—and signaling to the universe that you know your needs will be met on time and in time. Again, gratitude will shift us from fear and judgment to trust and love.

Think of a few items you have let go of (or are hesitating to let go of) and express your gratitude here:

I am grateful for ____
for____.

I am grateful for ____
for____.

I am grateful for ____
for____.

I am grateful for ____
for____.

I am grateful for ____
for____.

I am grateful for ____
for____.

I am grateful for ____
for____.

Intention

Let go of your items with the intention that they will serve someone else. You may say, "May this be used in loving service for someone else's highest and greatest good." When you imagine your items being put to good use serving someone else or bringing them joy, it makes it much easier to let go. You can give your items a better chance of finding a good home by making sure they are clean, in good repair, folded, and categorized.

Gratitude and intention make it so much easier to let go. And implementing these practices ensures we will experience the full benefits of decluttering: the point of clearing clutter is to free up space in our homes, our minds, and our hearts. If we are judging and fearful when we let go, we will not experience this lightness, but when we give with a grateful heart and clear intention to be in loving service, we will feel truly clutter-free inside and out.

Action Step:

Thank your items for serving you, and send them off with the intention that they serve someone else.

Trash, recycle, donate, and/or sell the items you have chosen to let go of. Get them out of the house—and the trunk of your car, which doesn't count as letting go!

Week 13: How to Declutter the Less Obvious—Hard-to-Let-Go-of—Types of Clutter

"Remove the emotional and physical clutter from your life so you can soar."

–Judith Orloff

In Week 7, we mentioned that there is obvious clutter and less obvious clutter. This week, we are going to explore the less obvious types of clutter. These may be objects that you would never have considered clutter before, and it's often the type of clutter that's most challenging to let go of. But this less obvious clutter also has the potential for the greatest benefit once we let go of it, because it's often the clutter that holds us back from manifesting our dreams.

All clutter—the things that are no longer loved or used—takes up space, demands your time and effort, and can get in your way. However, the true reason clutter holds you back is because most physical clutter is actually *emotional* clutter.

Underneath most clutter is a thought or limiting belief that elicits feelings of overwhelm, guilt, sadness, regret, or frustration, to name a few.

Here are some examples of physical clutter and their associated emotions:

- A gift you don't like but feel obligated to keep (resentment).
- An expensive purchase that you realize you will never use (guilt).
- An item that you are holding onto just in case __________ happens (fear).
- An object from a past romantic relationship (sadness, regret).

As you read this, did any items that are emotional clutter for you come to mind? Write about them below.

You can see how physical clutter is really emotional clutter—weighing on your heart and mind. If you let go of the emotional clutter, you have the opportunity to release the belief and feelings along with the object, freeing up space inside yourself for more love and joy.

Below are the most common types of less obvious or emotional clutter.

Rainy-Day Clutter

You know you have rainy-day clutter when you hear yourself saying, "I'm holding on to this item just in case?" In fact, Karen Kingston, author of *Clear Your Clutter With Feng Shui*, aptly calls this "just in case" clutter. Just in case I lose my job, get divorced, or don't have enough money to buy a new one... Here's an example: I'm going to hold on to this wrist brace just in case my child sprains their wrist again... Or I'm keeping these moving boxes from my last move just in case I have to move again...

Underneath all the rainy-day clutter is fear. Fear that we won't have something when we need it or fear of some negative scenario in the future—anticipating something bad that hasn't happened yet and may never happen. When we see or interact with these objects, it keeps our attention on a rainy day or a negative future scenario, focusing our attention on what we *don't* want, not what we *do* want. As Reverend Michael Beckwith, author of *Spiritual Liberation* says, "What we think about, we bring about." To manifest our desires the goal is to keep our attention on the things we *do* want in our lives.

Decluttering provides us with an opportunity to let go of these items and the fears they remind us of. As we're letting go, we can affirm to ourselves that all of our needs will be met on time and in time, in this way placing our attention on a positive outcome.

Someday/Maybe Clutter:

Someday/ maybe clutter is similar to rainy-day clutter, but a little different. For example: I'm keeping every little scrap of paper, egg carton, or ribbon because someday/maybe my child will use it for an art project...

I'm holding on to these books I have had for five years because someday/maybe I will read it..

Or, most common, I am holding on to these clothes because someday/ maybe I'll fit into them again...

Instead of holding on to the someday/maybe clutter, we are better off making choices from our present moment circumstances. Ask yourself: Is this item serving me now? Are clothes that are too tight serving me? Or do they make me feel bad when I look at them when I'm getting dressed in the morning?

You can also ask: What is in alignment with my current goals? Are these books still in alignment with my interests and pursuits today? Or are they tied to a version of me in the past?

We have found that so much clutter can be prevented when we allow ourselves to fully live in, accept, and embrace the present moment.

Unwanted Gifts, or Afraid-to-Hurt-Someone's-Feelings Clutter

This one is so tricky. Of course we all know that it really is the thought that counts, but we don't want to offend people who gave us a gift. Yet it can be really disempowering to live with things that we don't like and feel obligated to keep. It is actually better to tactfully let them go. In fact, we've found letting go of a gift that you don't love or use may be better for your relationship with the gift-giver—because when you hold onto it out of obligation, resentment builds...

The best way to address this kind of clutter is to be preemptive by graciously letting friends and family know you're currently paring down and simplifying your home—hint, hint. If they really want to give you something, then tell them you'd love an experience like a gift certificate to a restaurant, homemade cookies, or babysitting hours!

Remember: you can enjoy receiving the gift and appreciate the gift-giver, but you don't have to hold on to it forever.

Too-Expensive-to-Let-go-of Clutter

This is just what it sounds like! You spent a lot of money on something you don't use, and you can't stand the idea of wasting it. But holding on to it just ends up being a waste on two levels... If you aren't using it, it's actually a greater waste to keep it when someone else could use and enjoy it.

And if you are continuing to judge yourself for a "mistake" purchase or spending too much money, you're just wasting your precious energy. We can't change the past. Forgive yourself, learn from it, and move on.

Sentimental Clutter

This type of clutter often includes photos, letters, souvenirs, or children's things. Keep in mind that you don't need an abundance of objects to remind you of a meaningful time in your life. If the time in question is that special, you'll always be able to recapture those feelings just by recalling the memories. Be selective about which nostalgia items you keep—and remember that you can always take a picture of them and/or journal about the memory.

If you love the item, if it makes your heart sing, by all means keep it—but we often hold on to this type of clutter because we are afraid that if we let go, we will somehow lose a piece of ourselves or a memory. In truth, we don't need the object, because the experience is a part of us.

Also, we've found that the sentiment attached to objects may change over time. Check in with your sentimental items and make sure they still have the same meaning to you that they did before. And ask yourself: Does that sentiment still align with who I am today?

Inherited Clutter

This type of clutter is similar to unwanted gifts in that you may be keeping something you don't love or use out of obligation. But you are not responsible for other people's clutter—even your own family's. Of course, keep any inherited items you find useful and love. But anything else, especially if you don't like it or it has negative feelings or memories associated with it, let go or pass on to a family member who *will* cherish it. You have an opportunity to curate your family history in a way that makes you feel good and empowered.

When letting go of inherited clutter, I like to take a picture of it and send the photo to my relatives. I can ask whether anyone else in the family wants it, and if they don't, I can let it go. And if you are thinking, I need to save this for my children, ask yourself: Am I passing down a treasured heirloom, or am I really just passing down clutter that they won't love or use?

Action Step: Declutter Emotional "Less Obvious" Types of Clutter

The exercise below will help you discover any types of emotional clutter that may be weighing you down. This exercise can also help you identify clutter that's misaligned with your intentions and vision for your ideal life. For example, items from a previous relationship that may be holding you back from making space in your home and heart for a new relationship. Or an item tied to a limiting belief about lack that may be blocking you from manifesting wealth. Or clothes that don't fit that make you feel bad about yourself and dampen your motivation to achieve your health goals.

Find a quiet place to turn within. Close your eyes and take a few deep breaths. Ask your home for support in manifesting your desires. Visualize your ideal life. Ask whether there is anything in your home that is not serving your vision for your ideal life. Something may come up right away.

Write down anything that comes to mind.

____

____

____

____

____

____

____

____

____

____

____

____

If nothing comes to mind, open your eyes and look around your home to see if something stands out. You may also notice that something comes to mind in the next few hours or days. If something does come to mind, consider letting go of the object.

Week 14: Revisit Your Life Design

"Every aspect of your life is anchored energetically in your living space, so clearing clutter can completely transform your entire existence."

–Karen Kingston

As we've discussed, clutter keeps you stuck in the past. It's difficult to envision your ideal life—and be open to the opportunities, people, and energy that will support you in creating that life—if you are weighed down by the past. By letting go of items that are not loved or useful in your home, you will make space for the things that truly serve you, support your goals, and reflect your desires in this moment.

Clutter is another form of resistance—it distracts us from moving towards our goals. Decluttering brings you to the present moment and empowers you to take action.

Clutter creates stuck energy in your home, causing blocks in your life. When you declutter, you allow the energy to flow freely in your home, often resulting in good things flowing into your life

When you are deciding what to keep and what to let go of, ask yourself: Does this item support my goals? Is it in alignment with my highest vision for my future? If I were living my dream, would I keep this item? Does this item inspire the feelings I would feel if I were living my dream?

For the items you choose to let go of, do so with love and gratitude for bringing you to where you are now. As you make choices with a clear vision and a grateful heart, you are shaping your life.

Action Step: Declutter with Intention

Revisit your life design. Read your intentions about what you wish to manifest in your life. With these desires and goals in mind, declutter. As you determine whether to keep or let go of the item ask yourself: Would I keep this item if I were already living my dream? If my goals were already manifest?

Week 15: A Decluttering Secret

"How you relate to the issue is the issue."

–Drs. Ron and Mary Hulnick

How you clear clutter—meaning how you are with yourself as you clear—is often more important than what you ultimately choose to keep or let go of. The energy and intention you bring to the process of clearing clutter will influence the end results. If you are decluttering to create more love and peace in your home, then it makes sense to be loving with yourself as you clear, as opposed to judging yourself as wasteful or disorganized.

If you come from a place of curiosity, lightheartedness, and acceptance, as opposed to self-judgment or resistance, you will create more love and joy in your home.

To declutter from this place of acceptance, begin your decluttering with the question, "Which part of my home needs more love?"

Does any area come to mind?

If you find yourself judging yourself as you clear (and we all do) or engaging in negative self-talk, follow our four steps for handling judgment:

1. Observe: simply say to yourself, "Oh! There I am judging."

2. Forgive: forgive the judgment by saying, "I forgive myself for judging myself as disorganized, wasteful etc..."

3. Affirm: affirm something that is more true and aligned with your intentions, such as "the truth is I am gaining clarity about will best serve me. The truth is my life is about love, joy, abundance etc..."

4. Return to your clearing. Go back to the "doing," decluttering.

Action Step: What Areas Need More Love?

Begin decluttering the areas of your home that you identified as needing more love. As you declutter, if any judgments arise, use the four-step process.

Reflect on how your decluttering feels when you come from a place of love:

Week 16: How to Organize

"The easiest way to organize your stuff is to get rid of most of it."

–Joshua Fields Millburn

Remember that organizing comes after decluttering. Clutter cannot be organized. As we like to say, clutter in a pretty basket is still clutter!

You may prefer to wait until your entire home is decluttered before you start organizing, or if you have finished decluttering a room, you may wish to organize that room. Just keep in mind that if you organize a room before your entire home is decluttered, you may end up going back and adjusting. This results from the domino effect I described earlier. For example, if you declutter and organize your kitchen and then later declutter and organize your garage, you may decide to relocate some rarely used kitchen items (such as holiday dishes) into space you opened up in the garage so that you can free up the most accessible space in the kitchen for everyday items.

The key to organizing is to find a good home within your home for each and every item. A good home for an item is:

1. Clean and spacious.
2. Easily accessible.

Our items are happier and will stay in better shape when they are stored in a clean and spacious area. Also, a spacious area will make them more accessible. The goal is to make it very easy to return items to their home, otherwise we will avoid the task and not pick up.

Tips for Organizing:

1. Like with like in the location where you most often use it: Most of the time, it is best to store like items with like items in the location where we most often use them. We tend to do this naturally. For example, we store kitchen items in the kitchen, plates on one shelf, glasses on another etc.

However, If you are short on space, sometimes you will need to store things in another location to prioritize the things you use on a daily basis, e.g., you may store a roasting pan that you only use on Thanksgiving in the garage or attic to make space for the kitchen items you use more frequently.

2. Know your organizing style; make it easy: The key to developing the habit of putting things back where they belong is to make it very easy to do so! Know your organizing style. If you don't like to file, have neat piles. If a hanger is a bit too much effort, use hooks.

3. Don't over-organize: Over-organizing and over categorizing (color coding, alphabetizing) can also make it more difficult to put things away and is usually not sustainable. In a clutter-free space, you likely do not need to divide items into lots of containers or label each shelf or container. Unless of course, you adore organizing!

Other Tips:

1. Use what you have: It is more earth-friendly and saves money to repurpose containers, boxes, and other items you already own for storage. This is another reason to declutter first since you will likely free up storage items such as baskets or bins, thereby saving money.

2. Love your storage: If you do purchase new items, make sure they are held to the same standard as everything else in your home: loved and useful. Otherwise, the organizing items themselves become clutter!

3. Plan for temporary storage: Keep boxes or baskets on hand to house projects that may only be in your life for a period of time. Typically, we don't think of finding a home for these temporary projects and then they end up cluttering our space. For example, you could keep holiday cards, stamps, and pens in a basket, or your child's school art project in a bin. It is often helpful for these projects to be stored in a moveable bin because we may work on them in more than one location.

4. Plan ahead: Take a look at one type of item that tends to come in and out of your house and ensure there is a system in place to capture these items. What is your process for bills? Children's schoolwork? When you have a system in place and a designated location for the things you anticipate coming into your home, you will avoid clutter and disorganization.

Action Step: Give Your Items a Home

Once you have decluttered a room, or an area or category of items, find a good home within your home for the items you choose to keep. That is to say, organize!

Week 17: Limiting Beliefs

"Don't downgrade your dreams to match your reality. Upgrade your belief to match your vision."

–Lewis Howes

Manifestation is a result of aligning our thoughts, feelings, and actions with our desires. Our subconscious limiting beliefs can get in the way of this alignment. Limiting beliefs are thoughts we have about ourselves or the world that are in conflict with our intentions, and they get in the way of us realizing our goals and manifesting our ideal lives.

No matter how positive our thoughts, or how hard we work or how good we feel, if we have subconscious beliefs that undermine our goals, we will find it challenging, if not impossible, to manifest our heart's desires.

You have cleared clutter in your outer environment, now you have the opportunity to declutter your inner home—the thoughts or beliefs that are not loving or useful.

Limiting beliefs are based on fear, lack, and limitation, and more often than not they are subconscious.

Some examples of limiting beliefs are:

- I need to be perfect to be loved.
- Money is hard to come by.
- It is too late to ___________.
- There is not enough time.
- There is not enough to go around.
- I'm unlucky.
- I can't be in a relationship and be successful.
- When I have more time, money, love ___________. THEN I will be happy.
- I am not organized.
- You can't be creative and live clutter-free.

- I need to hold on to things I don't like just in case I don't have the money to buy things I do like.

Limiting beliefs stem from thoughts and opinions we attached to experiences from our past. When we repeat the thought over and over, it becomes habitual. These repeated thought patterns turn into "our story." The stories we make up about ourselves and the world tie us to our past and prevent us from freely and wholly being the most of who we are in each new moment.

Below are some common limiting beliefs. Put a check next to any that resonate:

- ❑ I need to be perfect to be loved.
- ❑ I am too old to ___________.
- ❑ It is too late to___________.
- ❑ There is not enough time to do what I want.
- ❑ When I have more time, money, love, or ______________, I will be happy.
- ❑ You have to struggle to be successful.
- ❑ Love always leads to loss.
- ❑ There is not enough to go around.
- ❑ Bad things always happen to me.
- ❑ I am unlucky.
- ❑ If I make a mistake I will be punished.
- ❑ If I fail, I will be alone.

- ❑ I won't be loved if I am not perfect.
- ❑ Other people will think I am ___________.
- ❑ I should never make mistakes.
- ❑ I can't be myself and be loved.
- ❑ I am only a good person if I put others' feelings ahead of my own.
- ❑ I am responsible for others' feelings.
- ❑ I have to fix ___________ about myself before I can be happy, wealthy, in love, etc.

- ❑ If I express how I really feel, I will lose the relationship.
- ❑ I can't be in a relationship and be successful.
- ❑ I am not pretty enough.
- ❑ I am not smart enough.

- ❑ I can't be kind and wealthy.

- ❑ You have to suffer to be rich.
- ❑ Money doesn't buy happiness.
- ❑ I can do what I love or I can make money, but I can't do both.
- ❑ Money is hard to come by.
- ❑ I never have money to spare.
- ❑ The rich get richer and the poor get poorer.
- ❑ Money is the root of all evil.
- ❑ More money, more problems.
- ❑ Money is not that important .
- ❑ I am not good with money.
- ❑ Money is scarce.
- ❑ Money needs to be held on to.
- ❑ Money doesn't buy happiness.

- ❑ I am not creative.
- ❑ I can't make money as an artist.
- ❑ I am not good at math.

- ❑ I am not organized.
- ❑ You can't be creative and live clutter free.
- ❑ Artists aren't organized .
- ❑ If I buy something expensive I have to keep it forever.

You may have found that you checked quite a few boxes—this is common! Most of us hold quite a number of limiting beliefs. Know that underneath every limiting belief is the overriding limiting belief that *I am unworthy of love, money, joy, and/ or any other good I desire.* Also know that most limiting beliefs are created in childhood. The limiting belief was a misperception of reality created by our childhood selves, most likely to protect us. In this regard, we can be grateful for the limiting belief for trying to help us. Just as we give thanks to the physical clutter for showing us what is no longer working (and release the objects) we can be grateful as we declutter the limiting beliefs. We can thank the part of us that was trying to keep us safe—and know that now our adult selves are here to keep us safe. We can be safe *and* be free of any limitations. We can be safe *and* live our best lives, fully expressed.

Limiting beliefs can be reflected in our homes. But before you turn to your home, the first step is to identify and reframe your limiting beliefs.

Action Step: Identify Limiting Beliefs

1. Are there any limiting beliefs you hold about your ability to achieve your vision for your ideal life? (Clues that you have limiting beliefs are when you catch yourself doubting or thinking of all the reasons you can't do something; also if you hear yourself saying, "I should, I'll never, I can't, I'm too ___________, I'm not ___________, I don't ___________, etc. These words are usually signals that you have a limiting belief.) Write down any limiting beliefs you may have about your goal.

2. Look for proof of how the limiting belief is false. For example, if you have the limiting belief that you are too old or it is too late to achieve your goal, yet you know someone or read a story about someone who achieved the same goal at your age, this disproves the limiting belief. Write down the example next to your new belief.

3. Next to each limiting belief, write a new belief. You may choose to write this in the form of an affirmation. You can also express gratitude for how this part of yourself may have been trying to protect you, but now it can let go, as you are here to choose a new belief.

Belief:

____

____

Examples that disprove the belief:

____

____

____

Gratitude for how the belief thought it was protecting you:

____

____

____

Reframes or new beliefs:

Belief:

Examples that disprove the belief:

Gratitude for how the belief thought it was protecting you:

Reframes or new belief:

Week 18: Limiting Beliefs Attached to Clutter

"Whatever you accomplish in life is a manifestation not as much of what you do, as of what you believe you deserve."
–Les Brown

Limiting beliefs can be reflected in your home through clutter, as we alluded to in Week 13. Clutter results from beliefs rooted in fear, lack, and limitation—i.e. limiting beliefs. If you find yourself holding onto an item that is not loved or useful, you will usually find that underneath your resistance to letting go of the object is a limiting belief.

Here are some common limiting beliefs attached to clutter:

- If I let go of something expensive, it means I am wasteful, or If I buy something expensive I have to keep it forever.
- I better keep this item I don't like because I don't deserve one I really do like.
- I better hold on to this item just in case (fill in the blank with whatever future needs you think will not be met).
- I need to be cluttered to be creative.
- If I let go of this sentimental object, I will lose a piece of myself, or I will lose my connection to the thing/person/place that it reminds me of.

Once you become aware of the reasons you are holding on to the clutter, you can affirm a new, positive belief. For example, you could say to yourself, "My needs will always be met on time and in time," "I am worthy and deserving of the good I desire," or "I am enjoying clarifying what works for me and what doesn't." You can then release the item (and the limiting belief) with gratitude for providing this opportunity to embrace beliefs that reflect and support a life you wish to manifest—a life of unconditional love and infinite resources.

If you cultivate the beliefs that you are worthy and whole and the universe is infinite and abundant you will gravitate towards the things you love and use—the things that reflect and support your highest vision for yourself, your home, and your life.

Action Step: Releasing Clutter Tied to Limiting Beliefs

1. Revisit your list of limiting beliefs that may be in the way of your realizing your goals.

2. Find a quiet place to turn within. Close your eyes and take a few deep breaths. Think about your vision for your ideal life. Ask yourself whether there is anything in your home that is attached to a limiting belief. Something may come up right away. Write down your thoughts here:

If nothing comes to mind, open your eyes and look around your home to see whether something stands out.

3. Consider letting go of the item with gratitude (for showing you what no longer works.) As you let go, affirm a new belief.

Week 19: Identify and Release Limiting Beliefs Reflected in Your Home

"Every time you replace a fearful thought with a loving thought, you make the world a better place."
–Denise Linn

It can be challenging to unearth limiting beliefs, because they are often unconscious. Fortunately, your home can help you bring them to light. In Week 1, we talked about how your home reflects your life. You completed an exercise to help you see how your home tells your story. Now you are going to look a little deeper to unearth the limiting beliefs behind the story.

Our homes are a reflection of our consciousness. Therefore, it is common for limiting beliefs to be reflected in our homes—but it can be a little tricky to spot them! It is much easier to see someone else's patterns. However, when you have a new awareness, you will start seeing them for yourself.

Here are some examples:

Reflection: A single woman looking for a relationship and every piece of art in her home depicts a lone woman looking sad.
Limiting belief: I can't be happy and whole until I am in a relationship.

Reflection: Living with many items that aren't loved or in disrepair.
Limiting beliefs: I don't deserve to have the best. I will never have a lot of money to buy beautiful things. My family never had a lot of money.

Reflection: A successful businessman whose bedroom resembles a college fraternity room.
Limiting beliefs: I don't deserve to invest in myself. I will care about my home someday when I settle down.

Reflection: A single woman in a half-decorated home.
Limiting beliefs: I don't deserve to invest in myself. If I am too independent, I won't meet someone.

Reflection: Couple living with unpacked moving boxes.
Limiting beliefs: If we settle down, we will be boring. The second I settle down, I will have to move. If I love my home too much, it will get taken away.

Reflection: Saving the best things for the future, such as the cloth napkins, the best china, favorite clothes, or candles.
Belief: An imagined future is more important than the present moment.

Reflection: Not fixing up a home because it is a rental.
Belief: I am not worthy of a nice home now. I am not worthy of investing in myself. I will be happy *when* I can own my own home.

Reflection: A bedroom that is also a home office.
Belief: I can't be successful in my career and be in a loving relationship.

Reflection: A bedroom with a treadmill in it.
Belief: I have to earn my time for rest and self-care.

Reflection: An adult woman's bedroom filled with stuffed animals, dolls, or other items that are more appropriate for a tween.
Belief: If I bring my full power to a relationship, I won't be loved or accepted. Relationships have always ended in loss (so I would rather not put myself out there.)

Reflection: Creative people living in a cluttered home.
Limiting belief: I need to be cluttered to be creative.

Reflection: A bedroom set up for one person when they would like to be in a relationship.
Limiting beliefs: I won't ever meet anyone. True love doesn't exist.

It is important to point out that these are examples of common limiting beliefs that we have experienced or clients have experienced. A treadmill in the bedroom or art depicting a single woman is not always tied to a limiting belief! Similar to the idea that what is clutter for one person is not clutter for another (because only you know what is loved and useful for you), only you will know whether these reflections in your home support your dreams and goals—thereby moving your forward- or reflect lack and limitation- keeping you right where you are.

The beauty of working on yourself through your home is that when the limiting beliefs are identified, they are on display three dimensionally—you can really see them! They are tangible and you get to do something about them. You can let go of the item that you are holding on to out of fear and limitation, or make a physical change in your home. For example, you can replace the art of the sad-looking women with images that depict a happy confident woman. You can let go of the items that you don't love while affirming the intention that you are manifesting the abundance to purchase things you really do love.

Action Step: Identify and Release Limiting Beliefs

Review your life design and think about your vision for your ideal home and life. Review your list of the limiting beliefs you identified. Next, take a look around your home with "fresh eyes." Do you see any limiting beliefs reflected in your home?

Make a list of any limiting beliefs you see reflected in your home:

What changes can you make in your home to undo these reflections of your subconscious beliefs?

How can you affirm a new belief in your home?

Consider removing, relocating, rearranging, or replacing the items. An example is relocating a home office in your bedroom to another part of your home and replacing it with a cozy place to read or a quiet place to meditate to support an intention of self-care or consistent spiritual practice.

How can you tell a new story?

Week 20: If You Can't Change It, Reframe It

"Simply with a change of mind you can change your life."
–Deepak Chopra

Sometimes we come across things in our home that are not loved, or that reflect a limiting belief, but that are very useful and can't be replaced right away. If an item is very useful and you cannot afford to replace it, it may be better to keep it, even if the item reflects a limiting belief or is not loved. For example, if you feel your sofa anchors a limiting belief about lack (i.e., you don't really love it, but you can't afford a new one), yet the sofa is the only place to sit down in your living area, then the absence of this sofa may actually reinforce the limiting belief more than keeping the sofa would.

In this case, if you can't change it, reframe it!

Look for what you do appreciate about the sofa (such as the dimensions or the color or even just the fact that it gives you a place to sit) and give thanks. You may also consider placing something you love on the sofa, such as a pillow or throw blanket. The loved item(s) will keep your attention on what you *do* want in your life (more things you love). Finally, you can find images of your dream sofa—again, placing your attention on what you desire—and in the meantime, thank your current sofa for being a placeholder for your new one that is now manifesting. Your gratitude will shift your relationship with the sofa.

You may also find that you love an item but it may not be aligned with your intentions. For example, you may desire a relationship and own a painting that you love that depicts a single woman. In this case, you may wish to relocate the painting to a different part of your home—e.g., since a bedroom is associated with love, you might move the piece from the bedroom to the living room. Or you may wish to balance the artwork by adding other artwork to the bedroom that depicts a happy couple. Another option is to reframe the artwork: you could set the intention that the artwork is an affirmation for love because finding love requires you to first be whole and happy on your own.

Action Step: Reframe

Make a list of any items in your home that are not loved but that you may choose to keep because they are useful, and also any items that reflect a limiting belief but that you prefer to keep because they are loved or useful. Under the item, write a reframe.

Item:
Reframe:

____

____

____

Item:
Reframe:

____

____

____

Item:
Reframe:

____

____

____

Make a habit of appreciating the items when they capture your attention. Affirm the reframe.

Week 21:
Check in with Artwork

"Our subconscious minds have no sense of humor, play no jokes and cannot tell the difference between reality and an imagined thought or image. What we continually think about eventually will manifest in our lives."

–Robert Collier

What you choose to place on the walls in your home will have a significant impact on the feel of your space. Therefore, it is important to make sure that you love how you decorate your walls. Wall decor tends to capture our attention, so it is a good idea to make sure you are placing your attention on things that align with your desires. As you look for limiting beliefs reflected in your home, a great place to start is by checking in with artwork.

When you are addressing conceptual art, it's important to tune in to your body. How your body responds is more important than how your mind logically interprets the piece. Your body will reveal your subconscious response.

Keep in mind that even though a piece of art may be perfectly lovely or interesting, it may not be in alignment with your current vision. If you love it but it is not supportive of where you are now, consider storing it or placing it in a location where it is not a daily focal point. If you don't love it and it is not a vibrational match for your current intentions, it is probably time to let it go.

Action Step: Tune in to Your Artwork

1. Stand in front of each item you have hanging on your walls and tune in to your thoughts, emotions, and body. What thoughts come to mind? Is the piece associated with a particular memory? What emotions does it elicit? How does your body respond? Do you take a deep breath and feel

expansive? Or do you feel depleted, or perhaps a nagging feeling near your core? Is the piece in alignment with your intentions? Does it support an abundant outlook, or does it reflect lack, limitation, or another limiting belief?

2. If the piece does not align with your intentions or does not inspire love, consider removing it.

Week 22: Check in with Photos

"Clutter is not just the stuff on your floor – it's anything that stands between you and the life you want to be living."

–Peter Walsh

As you address any personal photos you have on display, you can go through the same process as you did with artwork and ask similar questions. With photos, it is also important to tune in and see if the photo inspires love at this moment in your life.

Photos can bring us tremendous joy, but they can also keep us in the past or stir feelings of regret or longing or wishing things were different—all of which puts us in a state of resistance blocking manifestations.

There is a subtle distinction between whether an item brings you joy in the present moment by reminding you of the joyful time that used to be or prompts a loss of joy by reminding you of good things you no longer have. In the latter case, the item reflects a loss of joy. Instead of holding onto joy from the past, let go of the item and believe that this moment in your life offers the greatest possibilities for true joy. Trust that the best is yet to come.

Also keep in mind that photos are very personal—often more so than artwork. So be thoughtful about the location of your photos. Some photos you may wish to display in more private parts of your home, such as a bedroom, and some in more public areas like a living room. Placing photos in albums that you keep on bookshelves or on a coffee table can also create privacy while still keeping them easily accessible.

As with everything in your home, consider the purpose or intention of the room or area where you will display photos. For example, a bedroom's purpose is love and intimacy (which we will discuss in Week 28) and photos of in-laws or friends or children aren't particularly supportive of intimacy!

Action Step: Tune in to Your Photos

1. Hold or stand in front of the photos you have in your home. Tune in to your thoughts, emotions, and body. What thoughts come to mind? What emotions do the photos elicit? How does your body respond? Does the photo inspire love and make you happy in this moment in your life, or do you feel a longing for the past? Is the photo appropriate for the location (i.e., does it support the purpose and intention for the room)?

2. If the photo does not inspire present-moment happiness or is not aligned with the purpose of the room, consider letting it go or relocating it.

Week 23: Mirrors

"Our environment, the world in which we live and work, is a mirror of our attitudes and expectations."

–Earl Nightingale

A mirror can be a wonderful enhancement in your home. It can make a room feel larger, create a view, and lighten up a space. Since mirrors capture movement, they also have the ability to enliven and lift the energy in a room.

That said, it is important to pay attention to what a mirror is reflecting and whether it serves the purpose of the room. For example, a mirror that reflects a desirable outside view, a plant, or a beautiful work of art will be uplifting and inspiring. A mirror that reflects a bathroom, a long hallway or a low ceiling—not so much. For some people, mirrors in a bedroom are too energizing and therefore are not conducive to good sleep. In this case, the mirror may be better placed in a more social part of the house, such as a living room.

Keep in mind that mirrors double the energy of whatever they are reflecting, so it is important to check in to make sure the reflection is positive. We have seen mirrors reflecting a workspace; if you keep a tidy desk, this placement can work, but if a mirror reflects a desk that is messy or piled high with work, this placement will contribute to feelings of stress or overwhelm. This situation may also contribute to limiting beliefs, such as, "There is not enough time," "I will never catch up," or "I am just not an organized person."

Avoid placing mirrors such that you need to bend down to properly see yourself. Repeatedly bending down can cause stress on your body, and repeatedly seeing your image cut off or in fragments is not self-affirming.

Action Step: Check Your Reflections

Check in with the mirrors in your home. What are they reflecting? Are they in alignment with the purpose of the room?

Are there places in your home that would benefit from a mirror? Perhaps spaces that need more light or a better view, or small spaces that could be made to feel larger? Could you energize a space in your home by adding a mirror or doubling the energy of something positive, such as a plant, a loved work of art, or a beautiful outside view?

Week 24: Bring Your Dreams to Life in Your Home

"To be happy with yourself in the present moment while maintaining a dream of your future is a grand recipe for manifestation."

–*Joe Dispenza,* You Are the Placebo

You have identified and transformed limiting beliefs in your home. Now you can focus on bringing even more positive energy into your home by focusing on what you do desire. You can bring your dreams to life in your home by creating a physical intention.

A physical intention is simply a three-dimensional representation of your written intentions. Any object or groups of objects—i.e., photos, flowers, plants, books, or artwork—could serve as a physical intention.

The most important element of a physical intention is that it clearly reflects your goal and inspires the *feelings* you would experience if your dream were *already* manifest. This element is one of the most challenging parts of creating the life we desire—we must feel what it is we desire before it shows up in our life. For example, the fastest way to manifest abundance is to feel prosperous now. One of the reasons your home is such a powerful tool for manifestation is because your environment greatly influences your feelings.

Physical intentions are very personal. What represents love or abundance will vary greatly from person to person.

A physical intention can be quite literal.

Here are some examples:

- A physical intention for love could be a framed love poem.
- For wealth you could display a book titled Financial Freedom.
- A peace lily plant could reflect an intention for inner peace.

- You could hang a light or artwork that spells "manifest" to support all your intentions.

However, sometimes the best physical intentions are symbolic—or have personal meaning. Images and symbols, as opposed to words, appeal to the emotional, subconscious part of our brain; the stronger the feelings that are elicited the more the physical intention will capture your attention and maintain your focus.

Here are some examples:

- An image of floodgates opening can symbolize wealth pouring into your life,
- A clock can symbolize being in the right place and right time to meet your soulmate.

We had a client who had a horseshoe in his office to represent career success because he heard that another very successful businessman kept one in his office. We also had a client who had full-to-the-brim bowls of fruit in her kitchen, because for her nature's bounty represents prosperity.

Here is what happens when you place a physical intention in your home:

1. You change the energy in your home. Everything in our world is made up of moving atoms. When you place any physical object in your space, it has its own vibration and at the same time it is interacting with (and shifting) your own vibration and the energy in your space.

2. You support yourself in staying positively focused on your goal. Each time you walk by and see these displays of your dreams, you will be reminded of your goals.

3. You inspire the feeling of your desire manifest: whenever you take time to gaze upon and appreciate these objects, you will get an emotional charge. You will start to feel whatever it is you desire—successful, wealthy, romantic, etc.

When your thoughts, feelings, and actions align with your dreams, you put yourself in the best place to recognize, attract, and receive the opportunities that will support the realization of your goals.

Action Step: Create a Physical Intention

Make a physical intention:

1. Choose an object or group of objects that reflect your intentions and inspire the feeling of how you would feel if your goal were already realized.

2. Place the objects so they are a focal point in a room.

Make sure you love the objects. Even if an object perfectly represents your goal, if it does not bring you joy, it will not serve you!

Week 25: Arrange Your Home to Support Next Steps, Part 1

"You don't have to be the victim of your environment. You can also be the architect of it."
***–James Clear,* Atomic Habits**

As we explained previously, manifestations result from changing your thoughts, feelings, behavior, and subconscious beliefs. For the next two weeks we will focus on behavior. Realizing any goal requires taking consistent action steps. Your home can help!

You can design your environment to support and inspire the necessary action steps to move your goals forward. The idea is to behave in a way that puts you in the best possible place to access the law of attraction– meaning we stick to it! We consistently take positive steps towards our goals and build those habits we know support us in being the best we can be– even when it feels difficult, boring, or futile.

Thoughtfully chosen and well placed items in your home can serve as visual cues to support next steps. For example, if your goal is optimal health, and you decide your next step to realize that goal is to start your day with a green smoothie, you might relocate your blender from a hard-to-reach spot (such as the back of a corner cabinet) to your countertop. This simple change will make it easier to make the smoothie. If your goal is to be a writer, you might declutter your desk and create a comfortable, inspiring place to write. If your goal is to support better sleep, and action steps include getting to bed earlier and staying off screens, you may choose to remove the television from the bedroom and place a candle and beautiful books on your bedside table.

All of these visual cues will shift your energy so you are more motivated to complete the task at hand; overall, these reminders will make the experience of following through more enjoyable, which makes it more likely you will sustain the new habit or take the next step.

We will break this task down into two parts. First you will identify the action steps necessary to realize your goal. And then next week I will show you how to set up your home to support your next steps.

The key to a successful next step is to make sure it is clear and easy. This step is similar to organizing. When you organize your items, you choose a clearly defined home that is easily accessible, making it more likely you will consistently put the item back where it belongs. The same principle holds true for action steps: you are much more likely to follow though if the next step is clear and easy.

Action Step: Clarify Your Next Steps

1. Refer to your Life Design. Choose one goal or a habit from it that you wish to embrace.

____

____

____

2. Make a list of the action steps you can take to move this goal forward or pick an easy first step to building the habit.

____

____

____

____

____

____

____

____

____

____

3. Clarify your next action step by making it as specific, detailed, and easy as possible.

For example, if your goal is to publish a book, you might break it down into the following action steps:

1. Speak to a friend who has published a book to learn about the process.
2. Research online how to write a book proposal.
3. Organize your notes and ideas into a document.
4. Outline chapters.
5. Commit to a daily writing time.
6. Listen to an inspirational speaker or a daily meditation that gives you the confidence to move through any resistance.

If you find yourself hesitating to take the next step, chances are it is not clear and easy. You may need to break the step down further and/or be more specific. If your goal is to cook healthy meals at home and your first step is to gather recipes, you could narrow that step down as follows: ask my friend who loves cooking for her recipes, favorite cookbooks, or blogs.

The key is to make it very easy for yourself to take that first step towards your goal!

Week 26: Arrange Your Home to Support Next Steps, Part 2

"You are a product of your environment. So choose the environment that will best develop you toward your objective. Analyze your life in terms of its environment. Are the things around you helping you toward success - or are they holding you back?"

–W. Clement Stone

Now let's turn to your home!

Your home can support you in consistently following through with the habits, choices, and necessary steps to realize your goals.

Last week, you identified and simplified your next steps, so hopefully now you feel excited and confident to take action.

Design your environment to support your behavior and next steps:

1. Remove obstacles and reduce resistance.
2. Inspire the action step by creating clear visual cues.
3. Support the action by making it easy to follow through.
4. Elevate the experience—make it enjoyable by attaching a reward.

Remove Any Resistance

Resistance could be things in your environment that may get in the way of you taking your next step—physical clutter, for example. Keep in mind that sometimes you may need to "undo" something in your home that supports an unhelpful or old habit. For instance, if your default is to watch television in the bedroom, but your goal is greater intimacy with your partner or better sleep, you may need to remove the television.

Going back to the book-publishing example, let's say you find that your writing space faces your kitchen and this leads you to snack and procrastinate. In this case, you may want to change your view to one that supports you in staying focused on your writing.

Anticipate what may get in the way of following through, and then see if there is something you can change in your home to propel you past any resistance or blocks by inspiring different choices. Often, it is the seemingly small things that can have a profound effect on our ability to follow through.

Reflect on what gets in the way of your goal or habit. How did you procrastinate? Can you pinpoint what makes it challenging to take the next step?

Is there anything in your home that supports the undesirable pattern? Anything you can "undo" or remove?

Inspire the Next Step by Creating Clear Visual Cues

Create a visual cue to remind you to take action. For example, if your goal is to journal first thing in the morning, you could place your journal and pen on your bedside table. If your goal is to exercise, you could have your workout clothes laid out next to your bed.

Is there an inspiring visual cue or reminder your home can offer to inspire you to take action?

Support the Action Step

Make it easy to follow through on your action steps. You are more likely to take action if you can do so with minimal effort. Clear clutter, organize, and rearrange your space until it is easy to follow through with your action step.

I will avoid any task if it involves being cold. Since I live in the mountains, programming my heat so that it turns on thirty minutes before I need to get out of bed makes all the difference— otherwise, I may stay under the covers and skip my morning ritual! I also make it very easy to start my morning ritual (from bed) by having everything I need (guided meditation and journal) right next to me on my bedside table.

How can you support your action step? What changes might you need to make in your space?

Do you need to clear some clutter and organize to make it easier and more efficient? Would it help to move, add, or remove something?

Elevate the Experience—Make It Enjoyable!

You are more apt to take action again (and again) if you enjoy the process. Place a visual reward in the place where you take action.

Suppose you want to build the habit of reading books. You could create a reading nook. Choose a beautiful and loved item (object, photo, or artwork) as a focal point, or drape a loved and cozy blanket on the chair.

In the book-publishing example, you might create a writing area in your home. If you have a space in your home that you love and is comfortable, you will be more likely to follow through with the habit of writing daily. You might choose a very comfortable chair and have a favorite throw on hand. You could create an inspiring view that includes a work of art or inspirational quote. On your desk, you might place a candle, fresh flowers, or a favorite mug ready to be filled with a warm drink that feels like a treat.

Sometimes I avoid cooking dinner. Lighting candles and having flowers or a big bowl of fruit on my kitchen island makes the task more appealing. When I am really not in the mood to cook, I will listen to a podcast (a different type of reward).

How can you elevate the spaces where you will take action? What type of rewards, visual or otherwise, can you attach to the action step or behavior? Think about which textures, smells, sounds, and colors make you happy.

Action Step: Change Your Home to Support Next Steps

Thoughtfully chosen and well-placed items in your home can serve as visual reminders and shift your energy so you are more motivated to complete the task at hand and make the experience of following through more enjoyable.

Look at your reflections above and then create a space that clarifies, inspires, supports, and elevates the experience of taking your next steps.

Week 27: Live Your Dream

"One of the greatest strategies for success is to act as if you are already where you want to be."

–Jack Canfield

"Do you press the 'pause' button—the 'until' button—in life by saying 'I can't be happy until...'? Press the 'play' button and rejoice in the nowness of the moment."

–Michael B. Beckwith

Over the past two weeks, you clarified next steps and then designed a space to support your next steps. Now it is time to expand on these ideas and create a home that is energetically and visually so aligned with your dreams that you will find yourself living *inside* them. You will match the vibration of your home to the vibration of your desires. If you want to manifest abundance, you will start living abundantly and create abundant energy in your home; if you desire love, your home will vibrate with love; and so forth. You will expand your physical intentions so that they ripple out until your whole home reflects your goals.

This practice is often referred to as living *as if* your dream is already manifest. In truth, this can be difficult to achieve. How do you live prosperously if you are struggling to pay the bills? In the introduction we referred to this as the manifestation paradox. Your home is a powerful tool to overcome this dilemma.

We can find ways to truly and authentically live abundantly (or in love, or creatively, etc.) at home, or create space that feels abundant in our homes, even before we have manifested the money. This resulting experience in our homes—the physical, tangible, experiential reality—makes it much easier to authentically live *as if* and genuinely feel wealthy.

Here are some examples:

- Perhaps you can't afford the dream vacation at the five-star hotel right now, but you can bring some of the luxury of a hotel into your home by taking candlelit baths with your favorite bath salts or sleeping on a silk pillowcase or investing in high quality sheets.
- Dinners at expensive restaurants may not be in your budget, but shopping for fresh ingredients at the farmers market and preparing a home-cooked meal served on your best dishes might feel abundant.
- You might not (yet) have the romantic partner you dream of, but that doesn't need to stop you from loving yourself and creating a bedroom that is sensual and romantic.

Budget and space are two considerations that we have seen get in the way of living your dream. Here are few tips to overcome these challenges:

Start small: Keep in mind that you don't need to make over an entire room to start living your dream. If, for example, it is not in your budget right now to create a romantic bedroom for two, then start where you can. A clutter-free bedroom filled only with things that are loved and useful is enough to lift your vibration. You can make small changes a little at a time. Creating one area of beauty—a selection of love stories and fresh flowers by your bed that inspire you to be loving towards yourself by taking time to relax and read—is enough to put you in a place to draw the next love-filled thing into your life.

Decluttering will open up space: Remember that one of the reasons to declutter is to make space for your dreams—energetic *and* physical space. You may be surprised to find that after decluttering you have more space than you realize to dedicate to living your dream.

Repurpose rooms: Too often, entire areas in homes are unused for the majority of the year. If you don't use a formal dining or living area, turn it into a home office or art studio. Set up your home for how you spend your time 350 days of the year, not the other 15 where you may have overnight guests or entertain large groups. Live for yourself—authentically. Avoid "shoulds" when it comes to creating your ideal home. You can set up your home in any way that supports you living your dream now, even if it is unconventional. Focus on your present-moment needs and desires. Remember: you can always change it back!

A beautiful aspect of using our homes as a tool for manifesting is that we truly can start living our dream at home while we are waiting for our dream to materialize in the outer world. If your dream is to be a writer, musician, yoga practitioner, etc., you can create space and start writing, playing, and practicing. If your goal is greater wealth, chances are there are ways to live richly and abundantly at home right now. Perhaps home-cooked meals, lighting a fire, or diffusing aromas feels wealthy. Taking simple steps towards our goals and living in alignment with our soul's calling is what we call inspired everyday living, also the name of our online platform.

Hold a vision for the future (your intentions) and at the same time live as if your dream were already manifest—mainly by focusing on what ***is*** working and finding things to *love* and *appreciate* about your home (and yourself) now.

As you embody your highest self and vision for your life, the more you will free yourself from attachments to outcomes—and the less your happiness is dependent on these outcomes, the more likely those same outcomes will come to fruition.

Action Step: Change Your Home to Live Your Dream

Live your dream. How can you start living your dream now?

Perhaps the funds for the wealthy lifestyle you envision are still materializing, but in the meantime, how can you live abundantly *now*? Is it eating out once in a while or cooking a great meal at home for friends? Is it planning a trip or learning more about a different country?

Maybe your soulmate is still on the way, but how can you live in love *now*? Is it creating deeper connections with yourself or your friends? Is it feeling sexier and living more sensually?

What is the quality or value underneath your desire? How can you express these qualities in your home and bring them into your everyday living?

1. Revisit your life design. What are the top three areas of your life you would like to enhance? Or your top three goals?

____

____

____

2. How will you feel when these dreams are realized?

3. What changes can you make now to your home or lifestyle to start living your dream? How can you shift the energy in your home to align with your goals?

Lifestyle changes might include taking a bath each night, setting up a home office with the intention of working for yourself, starting writing your book now, setting up a romantic bedroom for two now, using your best dishes and linen napkins, buying fresh flowers each week (even a single stem rose, if budget is a concern), lighting the candles you have been saving for some day in the future, or wearing your best clothes now.

4. Begin implementing the changes you listed above.

Dwell in your dream. Turn your home into one big dreamboard so you're actually living *in* your dream.

Week 28: Healthy Home and Bedroom

"The greatest wealth is health."
–Virgil

While this journal is focused on decluttering and manifesting, we would be remiss if we did not mention the important connection between your home and your physical well-being. It's challenging to create success and enjoy our success if we aren't experiencing optimal health. Good health is undeniably the cornerstone for a good life. Like a sturdy foundation that supports a well-built structure, optimal physical health provides the stability necessary for individuals to thrive in every aspect of their lives.

Often the last thing we think about when decorating our homes is our physical health, when, indeed, it should be the first. What good is a beautiful room if the materials used to build, decorate, and care for it make us sick? Our homes should be a sanctuary, yet often they are just as stressful on our bodies as the outer world. In order to be a true refuge, it's important that our homes support our physical health.

We've all become increasingly aware of the numerous chemicals in our environment. That's why so many of us wash our fruits and vegetables, buy organic foods, and drink filtered water. But in addition to the food we eat and the water we drink, we also need to pay close attention to the materials we use to build, decorate, and clean our homes.

In many ways, your home is an extension of your body. What we have in our homes, how we clean them, and how we decorate are all decisions that affect our lives on a daily basis. In order for your home to nurture your physical well-being, you need to be just as mindful of what you put in your home as what you put in your body. For example, inhaling fumes from common household cleaning products that contain toxic chemicals can be just as bad for you as eating fruits and vegetables that were sprayed with pesticides.

Many common household items, including certain types of paint, finishes, carpeting, mattresses, curtains, dry cleaning, pressed wood (particleboard, MDF), and cleaning products, contain toxic chemicals. Many of the chemicals used in these household products, such as formaldehyde, toluene, and benzene, are Volatile Organic Compounds (VOCs) that, through a process called "off-gassing," release fumes into the air, causing indoor air pollution.

In fact, a study by the Environmental Protection Agency found that pollution inside a home could be two to five times higher than outside the home, even in large, industrialized cities.

Fortunately, there are many simple habits you can adopt and changes you can make to create a healthier home. Here are some simple steps that you could consider trying:

- Keep your home as dust free as possible. The less clutter, the less dust, and the easier it will be to clean your home. Use a vacuum with a HEPA (high-efficiency particulate air) filter to capture airborne particles. Not only is dust an allergen, but chemicals tend to bind to dust, polluting the air you breathe.
- Open your windows to ventilate your home on a regular basis. Opening windows creates a way for chemicals released from common household items to exit and fresh air to enter. Opening your windows for ten minutes a day can make a difference. Depending on your air quality, consider an air filter with a HEPA and carbon filter.
- Buy all-natural cleaning products. Household cleaning products are one of the leading causes of indoor air pollution, and studies have linked certain chemicals in conventional cleaning products with health risks. Look for non-toxic, environmentally safe household cleaning products. There is now a wide range of all-natural cleaning products available in stores. Also consider the less expensive and safest option of making your cleaning products by using common products found in most homes, such as baking soda, water and vinegar.
- Make a shoeless home. Shoes track in dirt and pesticides from outside onto our floors, where babies spend a great deal of time. Remove your shoes before entering your home. Avoid using pesticides and insecticides in your own home and yard.
- Choose a non-toxic dry cleaner, avoid dry cleaning, or at least unwrap and air out your dry cleaning before putting it in a bedroom closet.

- Avoid placing electronics in bedrooms. Computers, televisions, smartphones, and other electrical devices generate electric and magnetic fields, which can potentially cause health problems. Research is still ongoing, but it seems wise to avoid the risk.
- Limit your use of plastics for food and water consumption and storage. Use glass storage containers for food and do not heat food or liquids in plastic.
- Filter water. Although water quality varies depending on where you live, tap water can contain a host of contaminants, including chlorine, lead, and organic material. Install filters in your kitchen for drinking water and in your shower for water used to bathe.
- Use non-toxic body-care products. Our skin is our largest organ, and whatever we apply to our skin, we absorb.
- Sunlight. Sunlight can uplift our spirits. It is also an effective way to cleanse linens and blankets, killing dust mites. So open curtains and blinds during the day to let sunlight into your home, and hang carpets, sheets and blankets in the sun occasionally.
- An organizational system. You got this one! Studies show that stress negatively affects our health, and a lack of organization can contribute to stress. Creating a peaceful sanctuary at home by getting organized and eliminating clutter is another way to support your health.
- A pleasing view. Studies show that we relax more when we have a beautiful view. Don't worry if your home doesn't have a view. In the next few weeks we will be giving you tips for how to create a view.
- When purchasing new furniture for your home or office, consider investing in natural materials such as solid wood, untreated cotton, linen, wool, etc. Pressed wood, like particleboard or MDF, may contain chemicals like formaldehyde that can off-gas. Look for low- or no-VOC paints and finishes.
- Next time you buy new bedding, consider replacing sheets and pillows made of synthetic materials with organic bedding. If you don't buy organic, look for natural materials like linen or cotton, and consider avoiding anything that says "permanent press," "wrinkle free," or "stain repellents," because they're often treated with chemicals like formaldehyde. You may also consider buying a natural, organic mattress made of wool or natural rubber. And since mattresses also attract dust mites, which can trigger or

inflame allergies and asthma, try sealing your mattress in an allergy cover also made from natural materials.

If you are going to take some steps to improve the health of your home the best place to start is the bedroom. We spend a third of our lives in the bedroom and the bedroom is where our bodies and immune systems have a chance to take a break from outside stressors and replenish.

Also, sleep is fundamental to achieving any goal. It is challenging, if not impossible, to maintain clarity and focus, regulate our emotions, or have the motivation or energy to take purposeful action steps if we are short on sleep.

In addition to the healthy home steps you may wish to take in the bedroom, below are some tips and simple changes you can make to support a good night's sleep. You do not need to make all of these changes at once!

Tips for your bedroom:

- Position your bed so that you feel secure. It is human nature to feel more comfortable and safe when we can see who is approaching us. If possible, position your bed so that you have a view of the door but are not in its direct path. You will also feel more secure if you have a solid wall behind you. If you have a window behind you, then choose a solid headboard.
- Dedicate your bedroom to rest and romance. Ideally, anything that is not supporting sleep or romance will be kept in a different part of your home. In today's world, we are multitasking, and so are our bedrooms! These days, bedrooms not only house the bed, but more and more often they are also home offices, exercise rooms, and media rooms—it's no wonder many of us have a hard time sleeping. Give your mind and body a break. Computers, desks, televisions, and exercise equipment detract from the cozy, peaceful, romantic atmosphere you want to create in your bedroom. Imagine how hard it is to have a restful night's sleep or feel romantic when you're facing a desk piled with papers, bills, and a computer just waiting to be used. Your desk is like a big visual reminder of all the work that needs to be completed, emails to be answered, and bills to be paid. If possible, move anything that does not support sleep or intimacy to another room. If this is not possible, hide these objects when they're not in use in an armoire or closet.

- Maintain a Sense of Privacy. Try removing photographs of your friends, family and children from around the bed, or from the bedroom entirely. All those images are constantly reminding you of memories and relationships. They therefore have a very active energy. And you don't need to be reminded of your mother-in-law or your children during a romantic moment with your spouse. If you love photos, hang a photograph of you and your partner that reminds you both of a happy, loving moment you shared together.
- Declutter. It is challenging to rest and relax when your space is disordered. If possible, avoid under-the-bed storage, since it is best for the energy to circulate freely under beds and makes for easier cleaning.
- Promote harmony. You and your partner should both love your respective side of the bed. Check to make sure there is equality with regards to views from the bed, ease of getting in and out of bed, bedside tables, and lighting. If you are looking for a relationship, you should set up your bedroom for two. Energetically, by making space for two, you are setting a powerful intention. Subconsciously, a future partner will see there is room for them in your life.
- Limit your art and photographs. Only choose artwork that is conducive to sleep. And avoid hanging heavy art above the bed. It's hard for your body to fully relax with something heavy overhead.
- You may want to avoid having multiple mirrors or a very large mirror in the bedroom. Mirrors have a very active energy. Locate mirrors so that you do not see yourself when you are lying in bed.
- Avoid putting a television in your bedroom. Televisions tend to become the focal point of a room and can take over the room and replace connection and communication. Even when they are turned off, they have an active energy.
- Remove any artificial light. Cell phone chargers, DVRs, and alarm clocks all emit tiny lights that disrupt our sleep—it's best to remove electronics from the bedroom. Also make sure your blinds block any light coming from outside such as street lamps, headlights, etc. You will want to keep your room dark at night to help you sleep but bright in the day to lift your spirits. Choose window treatments that can be pulled back or up during the day and will block out light while you sleep.

- Have consistent bedtime rituals. Avoid watching TV and using your computer before bedtime. Also consider dimming lights a few hours before bedtime and taking a warm bath or shower. Keeping a notepad by your bed to write down any last minute things that are on your mind will also help you let go until morning. You may consider some form of nighttime ritual before bed; this could be as simple as thinking about all the things you are grateful for, taking a few deep breaths, or setting an intention or praying.

Action Step: Support Your Physical Health & Well-Being

What is one change in your home or habit you could embrace to support your physical health and well-being?

____

____

____

What is your next action step to implement this change or support the habit?

____

____

____

What is one step you can take to enhance your bedroom?

____

____

____

Take action now!

Week 29: View from Your Bed

"Never go to sleep without a request to your subconscious."

–Thomas Edison

What you see first and last upon waking leaves a very powerful impression on your subconscious. You begin and end your day in your bed, so this area of your home offers a special opportunity to support a positive outlook, reflect your intentions, and inspire good feelings.

What is your view from your bed? Is your view of a window? A television? A bathroom? A blank wall? Or artwork?

What thoughts and feelings does this view inspire?

Action Step: Align Your View from Your Bed with an Intention

Create an inspiring view from your bed that supports one of your intentions.

Keep in mind that the purpose of a bedroom is sleep and romance. As you are creating a view that reflects your intention, make sure that this view is not at odds with a good night's rest and/or your love life (e.g., if your intention is to manifest your dream job, images related to work may be too energizing before bed, but you may consider an image of an ideal vacation that the new job would fund).

Bonus: Uplift the Energy in Your Bedroom

Choose furniture, bedding, and colors that you love; create a beautiful and uplifting focal point with artwork or grouped items; add natural materials and bring nature indoors with flowers, plants, sunlight, nature objects; light candles; place a crystal in the bedroom; add soft materials with texture; diffuse essential oils; play music.

Week 30: Desk Position & View

"Even in the safest of circumstances, your nervous system relaxes more deeply when you have visual command of a room."

–Terah Kathryn Collins

The most comfortable and empowering placement for a desk is with a solid wall behind you and a view of the entrance to the room. In Feng Shui, this is referred to as the "power position." It is human nature to feel more comfortable and safe when we can see who is approaching us.

This placement also puts you in the best place to be open to, and greet, whatever opportunities may walk through the door. Even if you work from home, positioning your desk this way energetically puts you in a better place to attract and recognize opportunities. This position will also help you focus. For most of us, it is uncomfortable and distracting to not be able to see what is going on behind us. This is also true, even if we work at home alone. It's human nature to be more vigilant when we have our backs to a door.

Also consider your view from your desk. Since we tend to spend a fair amount of time at our desks, this is another area that provides an opportunity to anchor our intentions. You may choose artwork, an object, book, quote or photo that captures your intentions.

Don't forget about your screensaver! Your screensaver is another opportunity to stay positively tuned to your goals. Keep in mind that the image does not need to be a literal reflection, but rather can give you the feeling of how you would feel if you were living your dream (e.g., peaceful, abundant, thriving, or healthy).

Action Step: Put Yourself in the Power-Position and Create an Inspiring View

1. Try positioning your desk in the power position. If you like, you can test it out before moving your desk; try moving your desk chair to different spots throughout the room and sitting in it to see how you feel.

2. Check in with the view from your desk. How can you create an inspiring view? Consider anchoring your intentions by placing an object, art, or photo that reflects your intentions.

3. Choose a screensaver that inspires the feelings you would feel if your goal was already realized.

Week 31: View From Eating and Living Areas

"Design is coming to grips with one's real lifestyle, one's real place in the world. Rooms should not be put together for show but to nourish one's well-being."

–Albert Hadley

Check in with the views in your eating and living areas. Of course healthy food and proper digestion is essential for our well-being, as is having time to relax and unwind.

For eating areas, keep in mind that your view should be appetizing. This is not the best place to display artwork or photos that contain images that are unsettling or otherwise unappetizing. Candles or a bowl of fruit for a centerpiece will support mindful eating. Artwork that is in alignment with health and well-being can support your health goals.

In your living areas, your view should support relaxation. Often in living areas, the television is the focal point. If the purpose of the room is solely to watch television, this arrangement works. But if the room serves other purposes, such as together time with family or friends, or relaxation, consider not making the television a focal point. Televisions tend to control the room, even when they are turned off. Consider reorienting furniture so it is not solely facing the television. You could also place the TV in a cabinet or screen it off when not in use. If that's not an option, consider placing art above the television or a plant next to it so there's an additional focal point.

Also, just like with beds and desks, you will be more comfortable positioning your sofa so you have a view of the door to the room. In living areas, this is a more open and welcoming position. We wouldn't greet someone with our back to them, yet walking into the back of a couch can feel like being greeted by someone who has their back to you. Finally, this position also creates better energy flow in our homes. The goal is to feel that we can follow a meandering path through our home—as opposed to moving too quickly or being blocked by obstacles. We will discuss energy flow in depth in Week 36.

Action Step: Check Your Views from Your Eating and Living Areas

1. Check your views from your eating area. Is there something you could add or take away to create an appetizing view and encourage mindful eating?

2. Check your living area views. How can you support relaxation? Perhaps it is as simple as repositioning a piece of furniture and grouping loved items together to create a focal point.

Week 32: Your Front Door

"Think of your front entrance as the avenue of good fortune that attracts helpful people and opportunities into your home. Roll out the welcome mat, and make it entrancing."

***–Terah Kathryn Collins,* The Western Guide to Feng Shui**

The front entrance is essential to attracting and creating positive energy in your home (and therefore your life). The front entrance to your home is so important because this is the place where you greet the world. In Feng Shui, the front entrance is referred to as the "mouth of chi" because it is where the majority of energy (or chi) enters your home. Just as you take in air and sustenance through your mouth, your home takes in energy through its "mouth"—the front door. The goal is to allow as much positive energy as possible to flow into your home. The most welcoming and gracious way to greet someone is with a big smile. Make sure the front entrance of your home smiles too!

Here are a few things to keep in mind:

1. Make sure your entrance is well lit and that your address is clearly visible from the street. The goal is to make it easy for people (and, metaphorically, possibilities) to find you. Think about a retail shop. In order to attract customers, a store will make their entrance stand out and as appealing as possible. You can do the same with your home. Just think about attracting positive energy instead of customers.

2. Keep the entrance clutter-free. There should be no obstacles in your way, and the front door should open fully, symbolizing being fully open to opportunities. Avoid placing anything on the wall your door opens onto that might get damaged. For example, if there is artwork covered in glass on the wall and you cringe each time you

open your front door for fear of the door breaking the glass, this is not an uplifting and expansive way to enter your home. In fact, it is just the opposite: you will contract and feel anxious.

3. Create a meandering path to your front door. Ideally this path should be wide enough for two people to walk side by side. If your path is very straight, you can give it a meandering feel with plantings or potted plants. We are more comfortable and welcomed by paths that mimic nature.

4. Place something you love near the front door that lifts your energy. When you enter your home you're transitioning from the outer world to your inner world. Anything that captures your attention will encourage you to pause and shift gears as you enter your home. For example, fragrant flowers might encourage you to literally stop and smell the flowers, or a fountain might cause you to pause and listen to the water, or a doormat that says "welcome home" may make you smile. In addition to giving you a moment to transition, anything that brings you joy located by your front entrance will lift your energy, and then you will bring that positive energy into your home.

Action Step: Enhance Your Front Entrance

Consider the tips above and choose one change you can make to enhance the front entrance of your home:

____

____

____

____

____

____

As you make the change, imagine that you are ushering in positive energy to support you in manifesting your intention.

Week 33: Entryway and Purpose

"Behind our unremarkable front door waits the little world of our making- our home."

–Gretchen Rubin

What you see and feel when you enter your home sets a powerful intention. Your entryway is the place to welcome yourself home! Anything that is beautiful and loved will enhance this area. Perhaps you add a tree or plant or a lamp on a table that you can keep lit—making for an easy entrance at night—or you might hang a mirror to lift and circulate energy, or you may wish to install an inspiring piece of art in the entryway. All of these items can help set the tone for your home and even anchor your overall intention for your home and life.

Keep this area organized and clutter-free to support easy transitions for leaving and coming home. Make sure there is a place to easily hang coats, put down the mail and keys, and store other items. Also, you may want a place to sit down and take off your shoes.

Tips for the Entryway

1. Welcome yourself home: Add some loved objects, furniture, or art to your entryway so that you are greeted and inspired when you come home. What makes you feel welcomed and at home? Is it a lamp that stays lit so you have an easy transition in the dark? Or a soft rug underneath a chair or bench, so that when you take your shoes off your feet are warm? Maybe you keep fresh, fragrant flowers in this area and the beautiful smell welcomes you home. Or perhaps photos of family and friends create a sense of belonging.

2. Organized and functional: An entryway can quickly become a cluttered and disorganized space in your home. Think about the types of items you need access to when you leave your home and the things you may bring home. What storage do you need for these items? Likely, you will want a place to easily hang coats and put down the mail, keys, packages, and school backpacks or work bags. One of the principles of good organization is to anticipate and plan for the types of items that come in and out of your home and to ensure these items have a designated place to live.

Action Step: Enhance Your Entryway

Consider how you want to feel upon entering your home. Choose three words that capture your intention for your home.

1. ______________________________

2. ______________________________

3. ______________________________

How can you reflect these qualities and inspire these feelings each time you come and go? Make one simple change to your entryway to support your intention.

Week 34: Energy Balance and Flow

"Where attention goes energy flows"
–James Redfield, **The Celestine Prophecy**

This above quote, and variations of it, have become very popular in the world of the law of attraction because the words speak to an important principle of manifesting—a principle that we have been explaining throughout this workbook—namely, the importance of directing your energy (through your thoughts, feelings, and actions) towards what you desire

This expression has also been applied to Feng Shui, the 3000-year-old practice of balancing the energy in your home, to explain how energy moves through your space. You can track the flow of energy in your home by observing where your attention goes in your home.

The more you allow source energy to flow freely throughout your home, the more you increase the potential for success in your life.

Action Step: Track and Balance the Energy Flow in Your Home

Try this exercise to see how the energy flows in your home:

Walk through your front door and follow your gaze. Is your view obstructed by a wall? Does your attention move quickly through your space and out the back door or a large window? Are you drawn to a certain object, color, image, or area in your home?

____

____

____

You can also think of how a river would move through your home. If you opened your front door to a river of water, would the water rush through your home and out the other side? Would the river meander through all parts of your home? Are there areas where the water would pool and puddle?

Try closing your eyes in different areas of your home and see whether you can feel how the energy is moving (or not moving).

The goal is to have the energy from the mouth of chi (your front door) move through all parts of your home in a balanced way. The metaphorical river should be meandering and flowing—as opposed to rapid and turbulent or sluggish or stagnant. This river is a metaphor for your path and journey through life.

Write down places in your home where you noticed the energy seemed to either move too quickly or stagnate:

Places where energy stagnates:

Places where energy moves too quickly:

Choose energy enhancers from the list below to balance the energy in these places:

- A mirror or light to enliven a stagnate area.
- An orchid whose colorful flowers attract your attention to slow the energy down.
- Artwork that leads your eye to the right or left to "direct" energy flow into a certain area of your home.
- Lighting to lift the energy and direct your gaze upwards.
- A sparkling object, such as a round faceted crystal, to circulate the energy in all directions.
- A water feature that bubbles will also circulate the energy, whereas a fountain that flows in one direction will guide the energy.
- Area rugs or runners will slow down energy.

Week 35: Uplift the Energy: Beauty and the Five Senses

"The power of finding beauty in the humblest things makes home happy and life lovely."

–Louisa May Alcott

This week you will continue working with the energy in your home. Once the energy is balanced, you can think about attracting, aligning, and uplifting it.

One way to enhance the energy in your home is to engage the five senses.

Consciously engaging the five senses can relieve stress and help us stay mindful of the present moment. Which sights, sounds, tastes, smells, and textures are most pleasing for you?

You can also engage the five senses to elevate your goals and desires in a way that helps you maintain your focus.

Reflect on your Life Vision, or the overall intention for your home. How will you feel when you are living your dream? How will you feel in your ideal home? Next, add to your home the sights, sounds, tastes, smells, and textures that make you feel peaceful, abundant, creative, or whichever other feelings match your desires. In the same way that writing your intentions is a form of manifestation—you take the unseen world (your thoughts) and make them visible and tangible on paper—when your home engages your senses in a way that makes you feel what it is you desire, you are bringing your dreams into reality in an experiential and tangible way. The more you can embody your future self living your dream the more you will recognize the opportunities and behave in a way that moves you closer towards your goals.

Consider creating beauty in your home. Anything that is beautiful to you will attract positive energy and uplift the energy in your home. Create focal points of beauty that you (and the energy) are drawn to.

The more beauty you create in your home, the more inclined you will be to pause, take a breath, and appreciate life as you go about your day. Inhaling beauty inspires presence.

Action Step: Balance and Uplift the Energy in Your Home

1. Add some more energy enhancers (see list below) to your home to attract and uplift the energy.

2. Consider your intentions. Raise and align the vibration of your home with your intentions. For example, if you wish for more peace, how can you stimulate the five senses in a way that brings a peaceful energy into your home.

Intentions: How will you feel when your intentions are manifest?

____

____

____

Which sights, sounds, taste, smells, and textures make you feel this way?

3. At the very least, make sure you have at least one thing that is beautiful to you to feast your eyes on in every room. It could be as simple as a treasured book, a single-stem flower in a vase, or a bowl of fruit.

Energy enhancers to attract and uplift the energy in your home:

- Keep your home clutter-free: clutter stagnates energy.
- Live with what you love: one of the best ways to uplift the energy in your home is love everything in it.
- Highlight beautiful items.
- Let in sunshine and fresh air.
- Plants and fresh flowers.
- Nature objects, such as seashells, river rocks, or pinecones.
- Colors that you love—you can paint rooms or a single wall, or have accent colors by adding throws, pillows, artwork, etc.
- Light up your home: electric lights, nightlights, candles, and fire can all lift energy.
- Anything that stimulates one of the five senses: soft or textural fabrics, throw blankets, pillows. Bowls of fruit. Fragrant flowers or diffused essential oils. Beautiful, shiny, sparkling objects. Music.

Week 36: Everything Is Energy

"We live as ripples of energy in the vast ocean of energy."
–Deepak Chopra

All of the objects in your home are "alive" with energy. They are made up of moving atoms that result in their own unique vibration. These objects are also alive in the way that they spark memories, thoughts, and feelings.

Everything in your home is either lifting you up, bringing you down, or not doing much of anything. Choose to live in love. Surround yourself with things that make your heart sing.

By observing your body's response to an item, as well as your thoughts and feelings, you will know which objects lift your energy and create love and joy in your home and life—and which don't.

When you choose love inside your home, you also inspire love outside your home. You carry this positive energy with you beyond your own four walls and out into the world where it will serve to uplift and inspire others to live in love, and attract even more love and joy into your own life.

Action Step: Check in Again

Now that you have a deeper understanding and are tuning into the energy in your home, revisit objects and art. Stand in front of them and see if they lift you up, bring you down, or are neutral. Are there any items to edit or relocate?

Week 37: Purpose and Function

"Design is a plan for arranging elements in such a way as to best accomplish a particular purpose."

–Charles Eames

A clutter-free and organized home is certainly more functional than a cluttered and disorganized home. You can go even further by making sure your rooms serve their purpose. Having a home that functions well also contributes to the positive energy in your home.

The more empowered you are to fulfill your everyday routines with grace and ease, the better you will feel, and the better your home will feel.

Action Step: Clarify Purpose and Maximize Function

Make a list of the rooms (or areas) in your home and the activities that each room (or space) needs to support. For example, you might write kitchen and then underneath that list preparing meals, mindful eating, and homework area for the children.

Room:

____

Activities:

____

____

____

____

____

Room:

Activities:

Room:

Activities:

Room:

Activities:

____

____

____

____

____

____

____

Room:

____

Activities:

____

____

____

____

____

____

____

Next, spend some time in each room on your list and see if the room is arranged and organized in a way that supports the activities that you listed.

What simple change could you make so that the room functions well and serves its purpose more easily? An example might be placing a reading light near a comfortable chair, placing a basket near the kitchen table to collect kids' homework and artwork to make dinner prep easier, adding a puzzle or game table to your living area, installing kid-height hooks in your mudroom, or adding a bench to sit on and take off shoes.

Week 38: Comfort and Stress Triggers

"Real comfort, visual and physical, is vital to every room."
–Mark Hampton

Creating beauty in our homes is important, because beauty inspires joy and an awareness of our connection to our higher selves. However, sometimes we can get overly hung up on how to decorate our homes. Keep in mind that there is great peace, joy, and freedom to be found in an organized and functional home. A clutter-free and purposeful home can be your foundation. You can always go back later and beautify.

Also keep in mind that, at times, beauty and comfort may be at odds. The goal is to surround ourselves with beautiful things, but not at the expense of being comfortable in your own home. Depending on your lifestyle and whom you share your home with, an expensive fragile object or a white upholstered sofa may cause you to be on edge in your own home for fear of the object breaking or the sofa getting stained. The same could hold true for fine china or stemware.

Keep an eye out for things that cause actual discomfort in your space. Are there sharp corners or edges that you or other members of your household repeatedly bump into, causing stubbed toes, scratches, or bruises?

Sometimes the things that put us on edge and take away from our feeling of comfort do not cause actual harm, but instead trigger a stress response or that feeling of being on edge. In these cases, our subconscious will register a threat before our mind has time to override it with logic. The initial subconscious response will contribute to unease in your home.

Here are some common examples of things that can put us on edge:

- Heavy pots hanging overhead
- Exposed knives
- A chandelier over a thin glass table
- A glass door/ coffee table you can run into

- A cactus
- Heavy art or a heavy light fixture over a bed
- A candle close to fabric such as curtain
- Ceramic or a glass vase on a thin ledge
- Fragile items in a stuck drawer
- Dishes stacked too high
- Too much glassware shoved together in a cabinet
- Art hanging behind a door with no doorstop
- Any door that will slam into another door or object
- A glass candle holder on a bathtub caddy
- A heavy soapdish in the shower on a slippery narrow ledge

Action Step: Prioritize Comfort

1. Do you recognize any patterns in your home where someone frequently bumps into something or is frustrated trying to negotiate a task? These frustrations and minor bumps and bruises will often set off a chain reaction that leads to arguments or stress.

Is there a simple change you can make to address these concerns?

2. Is there anything in your home that may not cause actual harm but that seems to nag at you and create a feeling of unease?

Can you ameliorate these feelings by rearranging or removing something?

3. Consider making any changes you identified.

The one place we should always feel comfortable and at home is in our home!

Week 39: Views of the Outside World

"I live in a very small house, but my windows look out on a very large world."

–Confucius

In previous weeks, we talked about the importance of checking the views inside your home, particularly from the places you spend a great deal of time, such as your bed or desk. Also, consider your view of the outside world. The views from our homes have a tendency to influence our outlook on the world around us.

You will allow the good you desire to manifest more freely when you see the world as abundant and filled with infinite possibilities. Therefore, your views of the outside world should be pleasing. Also, studies show that we relax more when we have a beautiful view.

If your home does not have a great view, you can create one inside your home with artwork or mirrors—and outside your home with window boxes or landscaping. Also consider bottom-up shades, which are a great solution to hide unattractive views while still letting sunshine into your home.

Remember: if you can't change it, reframe it. Find a way to put a positive spin on an unattractive view. I will always remember a Feng Shui teacher sharing a story about a client who was discouraged by the security bars on her windows. She painted the bars gold, and every time she looked at them, she thought about her prosperous "bars of gold" I found myself in a similar situation in a ground floor apartment with security bars that had a decorative upward-spiral motif. I painted them white and added climbing jasmine—a smell I think is heavenly. Each time I looked at the bars, I thought of my connection to something greater.

Action Step: Create a Positive View of the Outside World

1. What are your views of the outside world from inside your home?

2. Are there simple changes you can make to transform an undesirable view? If not, how can you reframe your current view?

View:

Simple change:

Reframe:

View:

Simple change:

Reframe:

View:

Simple change:

Reframe:

Week 40: Cleaning

"A clean house is a happy house."
–Louisa May Alcott

Bringing mindfulness to cleaning transforms it from a mundane household chore into a meaningful ritual, elevating it from a routine task to an act of self-care and love. As you sweep, dust, wipe surfaces, or wash dishes, each activity becomes an opportunity to anchor your awareness in the present moment. The repetitive nature of housework lends itself to a natural rhythm that can turn cleaning into a moving meditation. This intentional focus not only brings attention to the physical environment but also nurtures a state-of-being where you prioritize the well-being of your home and the people within it.

As an additional act of self-care and caring for those we live with, we prefer to use all-natural cleaning products or even make our own cleaning products.

Most natural cleaning products are biodegradable, nontoxic, chlorine-free, and petroleum-free—all good for the planet, but also very good for you. Or for the least expensive and natural option with a quick search online you can find numerous simple DIY recipes.

Cleaning with all natural ingredients makes the process so much more enjoyable and healthier!

Action Step: Clean with Intention

Instead of viewing cleaning as a chore to complete quickly, consider it an opportunity to be fully present. Allow yourself to appreciate the order and fresh energy you're creating in your living space. You can also express your gratitude for your home and all the ways it serves you; mindfully caring for your home cultivates a greater sense of connection to your environment.

You may also consider setting a specific intention as you clean, such as cleaning your children's room to remove dust and allergens giving them a healthier place to rest and restore their bodies, or cleaning the bedroom with the intention of bringing more romance into your life (it's hard to be romantic when there's a pile of laundry on the bed!), or cleaning your front entrance to symbolically welcome new people and opportunities into your life.

Week 41: Clear the Energy

"Energy is Everything, including you,
When your energy flows freely,
your life flows easily"
***–Hazel Butterworth,* Energy is Everything**

There is another type of clutter that you can't see or touch: energetic clutter. While you can't see stuck energy, its impact can be just as significant as physical clutter in terms of being a block to the good things you desire.

Every space holds energy. Even though you can't see it, chances are you've sensed it. Maybe you've walked into a room that looked beautiful but somehow just didn't feel right. Or perhaps you've been in a space that was decorated poorly or not to your taste but you immediately felt good and comfortable. In both instances, you were probably tuning into the energy of the space.

Rooms can hold the energy of all the events, emotions, people, and activities that have taken place in the space before. In order to have a fresh start, and create more harmony, peace, and positive energy in your surroundings, it can be helpful to clear the energy periodically.

Have you ever referred to the need to "clear the air," or said something has a "good vibe," or after witnessing an argument stated, "you could cut the tension in the room with a knife"? Or perhaps you've even simply said that a place had "good energy." Many commonly used expressions indicate that we intuitively understand that buildings and places can have a certain vibration or feel.

So whenever you feel the need to "clear the air," clear the air!

Action Step: Clear the Energy

Below are a few ways to clear the energy in your home. Choose one and clear the energy!

- Allow sunshine and fresh air in with intention. Sunshine and fresh air clear stagnant energy (and improve indoor air quality). Just by opening windows with the intention of refreshing your space, you can clear the energy.
- Clean your home with intention. Dusting, wiping, and vacuuming with intention will clear stagnant energy. As you clean, ask that any energy that is not serving you be released and that positive, joyful, abundant energy fill your space.
- Cleanse the space with sound or fragrance. Similar to sacred space clearing rituals performed in many cultures, you can use sound or a fragrance to address areas that have stagnant energy. This is especially helpful if you have already decluttered and cleaned your home and something still doesn't feel quite right. Trust your intuition. For example, you can spray essential oils like peppermint or lemon mixed in water or play music or an instrument to clear the energy in areas that feel stagnant. For more details about energy cleansing we recommend Denise Linn's book, *Sacred Space*.

Week 42:
Clear Inner Clutter

"If you don't pay appropriate attention to what has your attention, it will take more of your attention than it deserves."

– *David Allen,* Getting Things Done

Inner clutter is another kind of clutter you can't see or touch. Inner clutter are all the thoughts that distract us from being in the present moment, from what we need to pick up at the grocery store for dinner to a long-held dream and everything in between. Inner clutter is the running to-do list in our heads, our hopes and dreams, worries about the future, and ruminations about the past.

All of these thoughts circulating in our heads can be just as much of a burden as physical clutter, affecting our ability to be present and free to enjoy our life and our ability to think clearly and focus.

Just like when our homes are so cluttered that it makes it difficult to find things or relax, our minds can get so cluttered that we are too overwhelmed to think straight, see clearly, or envision our ideal future.

Clearing inner clutter is a similar process to clearing physical clutter. When we clear physical clutter, the essential first step is to entirely empty the space. We take everything out of the cabinet or drawer. Only when we have taken everything out can we truly address each item to determine whether it is useful or loved. We need to do the same with inner clutter. Take everything out of our minds. We can do this by writing down all our thoughts on paper. Only then can we begin looking at each thought, desire, and goal and decide whether it is truly useful, loved, and in alignment with our highest vision for our life at this moment in time.

Action Step: Clear Inner Clutter

1. Sit down with pen and paper and spend 15–20 minutes writing down everything that is on your mind. Everything. Include thoughts about errands you need to run, your most heartfelt dreams, and everything in between.

2. Declutter. Look at each item on your list and ask yourself whether following through with whatever action is required is really necessary or useful? Would you love to follow through? In other words, you are seeing whether there is anything you don't need to do or don't want to do. For anything you realize you wouldn't absolutely love doing or isn't necessary, cross it off the list. Leave only the things that need to be done (useful things) and the things you love (that feed you and that you want to do).

3. Organize the thoughts you've chosen to keep.

We find the best way to organize our thoughts is by making lists. Digital lists are often best because we are continuously refining and moving items around.

Write any given day's high-priority tasks on a piece of paper.

Time-specific items can go directly on your calendar.

Here are some examples of lists we use:

To-do list: Single-step action items that you are committed to completing in the near future.

Project list: Projects that require multiple steps (next steps for a project can move onto a to-do list).

Wish list: Items we may want to purchase. Writing down the things we wish to purchase keeps us from making impulse buys. Usually, when we revisit the list after a period of time, we can't recall why we even thought we needed the item! (Using a particular store's shopping cart, save-for-later feature, or favorites also works.)

Practices & habits: This list we use for ongoing goals.

Ideas and Insights: This list is just what it sounds like! In addition to creative ideas, we will also write down any self-growth learnings or personal epiphanies.

Someday/maybe list: We also use *Getting Things Done* author David Allen's "someday maybe list." This list is for the things we may or may not ever do, such as visit Greenland, learn how to play the guitar, or write a book. This list is key to freeing up your inner clutter; since we aren't sure whether or not we will commit to the task, our brains will especially hold on to these thoughts.

Goals and dreams: Your dreams are likely already captured in your Life Design. Your Life Design will inform your goals list, which will inform your project list and even your to-do list. In this way, everything you do, even the smallest of tasks, is tied to a larger purpose. This process will keep you off the proverbial treadmill and instead propel you towards your higher vision for your life.

Keep adding to these lists as new things come up and refer to them daily so that you can choose where you will place your attention, time, and energy.

Chances are you now feel so much better! We usually find we have less to do than we thought—we were just recycling the same thoughts over and over. Often, the anxiety and overwhelm stems from indecision and worry that we are forgetting something. Once you have emptied your mind and organized on paper, you can relax and enjoy the moment.

Week 43: Habits to Prevent Clutter

The goal is not to become an expert at decluttering, but rather to stop accumulating clutter in the first place!
–Inspired Everyday Living

We are always changing—growing, learning, and becoming more of who we are. Our homes need to change too so that they reflect our new interests, goals, and values. For this reason, there will always be some degree of things moving in and out of our lives. However, once you have decluttered your home top to bottom and addressed each and every object, you should never go back to being as cluttered as you were before. The key to staying clutter-free is to embrace habits that prevent clutter.

Habits to Prevent Clutter

1. Ask before you buy. Before you make a purchase, ask yourself questions such as,

- Is it loved or useful?
- Could I borrow it? Rent it? Do without? Do I already own something that can fulfill this same purpose?
- How much of my time will this item require? (Keep in mind the time it takes to learn how to use it, install it, clean it, etc.) Do I have the time?
- Do I need someone else to help me set it up? How much of their time or my money will this take?
- Will it last? Is it high quality, and is the style timeless?
- Is it healthy for my body, my home, and the earth?
- Do I have a place to keep it?
- Will it replace something? Do I have time to find a home for what this is replacing? (i.e. drive to the charity/mail it/recycle it, etc.)

- What kind of project might this item lead to?
- Is it worth the investment of my precious energy?

2. Be mindful about the choices you make outside your home. Refuse to take anything home that is not loved or useful, whether it is a freebie, a flyer, or something you purchase. A lot of clutter results from choices we make when we are away from home—our goal is to not even let it in the door! You will find yourself getting creative about how to cut down on the clutter.

Here are some examples:

- If a flyer is left on your car, look for a trash can
- Someone hands you a business card—take a picture instead of accepting it or put directly into your contacts
- Ask for an email receipt
- Bring your own bag to stores—not just the grocery store
- Sort mail by your recycle bin
- Refuse freebies and samples (unless it's for a product you love and use)

3. Keep a "to-buy" or "wish" list. When we write down what we would like to buy, we often satisfy the need to have it. We sort of trick our subconscious into feeling like we already have it. The feeling of "I have to have it" subsides because the act of writing it down makes it seem like it will happen. We are then able to be more clear-headed when we make a choice at a later time. Part of our desire to have things has to do with control—we want to *be able to have it* more than we actually want to have it.

The wish-list works really well with kids. Create a wish list every time they ask for something on a shopping trip. Seeing you write it down appeases their need.

4. Wait a month before buying an item. Place it on your list. It is amazing what becomes irrelevant and unnecessary after a month. You may even find yourself forgetting why you felt you needed it in the first place, and why the need to buy it became the focus of your attention, and therefore, your energy.

5. Maintain. Build decluttering into your daily, weekly, seasonal rhythms. If you consistently stay on top of it and do a clutter check, you shouldn't have to spend too much time decluttering.

Action Step: Adopt Habits to Prevent Clutter

Reflect on how clutter tends to accumulate in your home and life? Is it from purchases, not having systems in place, indecisiveness, fatigue?

Which habit will best prevent this type of clutter?

Put this habit into practice! How can you support yourself in following through? For example, if your clutter stems from purchases, make a list in your phone of the questions you can ask yourself before making a purchase. Next time you have the impulse to buy something, ask yourself those questions.

Week 44: Habits to Stay Organized

> ***"Successful organizing forces you to look at the big picture, not one small section of the frame, so that the system you design will be complete."***
> ***–Julie Morgenstern,* Organizing from the Inside Out**

There is a difference between clutter (things that are not loved or useful) and items we do love and use but haven't put back in their homes. Sometimes, our home may look cluttered and messy, but in fact it may just be that the things we love and use aren't put away.

Here are some habits to adopt to stay organized:

1. Make it easy to put things away. Make sure you have a designated place to store your things when they are not in use. Make it easy to put things back, or it won't happen.

2. Think ahead and create systems. Anticipate what type of items come into your life and make a system to contain it. Is it children's artwork or schoolwork? Are you involved in creative projects? Do you tend to accumulate paper? Make sure you have a plan for how to efficiently process the loved and useful things that come into your home.

3. Self care and time management. A lot of disorganization results when we are tired and over-scheduled. Build in time not just for the activity, like baking cookies, but also the time to clean up and put things away. Rushing tends to create a little chaos. Schedule transition time from one activity to the next or from work to cooking or work to playing with the kids.

4. Get in the habit of making choices. Often, clutter and disorganization is a result of indecision, i.e., keeping the price tags on something because you don't know whether you will keep it, walking around with an item and then eventually dumping it on a table or stashing it in a drawer.

The more you practice making a choice, the less clutter accumulates, and the more your fear of making the wrong decision subsides.

The choice is: Am I keeping this? And if so, where?

Below are some examples of choices we can make to prevent clutter and disorganization:

- When your child brings home artwork from school, decide right away whether you will keep it and, if so, find a home for it. Avoid adding it to the pile on the dining table thinking you'll deal with it later.
- As soon as you get your mail, go through it and decide what you need to keep and what's junk. Don't let it stack up to the point where going through the mail becomes a daunting, time-consuming task.
- When you buy something and bring it home, decide whether you will keep it or return it (hint: if you find yourself hesitating before cutting off the price tag, chances are you aren't committed). If you're having second thoughts, return it right away.
- Any time you pick up a piece of paper in your office, make a decision rather than just moving it to a different pile. Either throw it away or file it. If you can't make a decision because you need more information first, then create a designated spot for things that should be dealt with later.
- Go through stacks of books and magazines and decide right now whether you will really read them. If not, recycle or donate them (tip: many magazine articles are available online, so most likely you'll be able to find the information you want if you change your mind later).
- When you find yourself continually putting on a certain piece of clothing, but then taking it off again, be honest with yourself—are you ever going to wear it? Before you hang it up again, make a decision.
- When you download photos from your phone or camera, decide right then which ones you will keep and which ones you will delete.
- Decide right after you read an email whether you will delete it or archive it or whether it requires an action. Email inbox clutter is always a result of not making a choice.

Making a choice prevents mental clutter, too. For example:

- If you receive an invitation. Decide right away whether you will attend the party and RSVP (you can always change your mind later if plans need to change).
- Before you put something on your to-do list, decide whether it is something worthwhile to follow through on.

Action Step: Adopt Habits to Stay Organized

1. Reflect on your organizational habits. If things are continually left out in your home, consider the cause: do you need a system, make it easier to put away, is it the result of not building in transition times, fatigue, or not making a choice?

2. What adjustments can you make in your home or which habits could you embrace?

Week 45: Three Inner Keys to Manifesting

"The future belongs to those who believe in the beauty of their dreams."

–Eleanor Roosevelt

In addition to creating an environment that is a fertile ground to sow the seeds of your dreams, you can also cultivate your inner home to support your manifestations. There are three practices that will support you in realizing your goals.

Three Inner Keys to Manifesting

1. Maintain a clear positive focus (avoid split energy)
2. Unwavering faith
3. Let go

Maintain a Clear Positive Focus (Avoid Split Energy)

One of the keys to manifesting is to keep your thoughts and attention on positive outcomes. It is important to direct your energy (through your thoughts, feelings, and actions) towards what it is you desire (as opposed to the absence of your desires.)

A lack of clarity and focus results in what Esther and Jerry Hicks, in their book *Ask and It Is Given*, refer to as "split energy."

Split energy is a result of focusing on your desires and the absence of your desires at the same time. In other words, putting your attention on what you want and at the same time putting your attention on how you don't have it right now.

Here is an example: You might be feeling and thinking "I am really ready for wealth to manifest in my life and feel really good about the intentions I have set and the action steps I am taking." But then you may hear yourself say to a friend, "I have just been under so much financial stress the past few years, and it is so exhausting. It is really time for a shift. I hope something good will happen soon."

This is an example of split energy. While you are talking about your desire—for more wealth—there is a lot of attention on where you have been (the past) and on the fact that the money hasn't manifested in your life yet.

It is not possible to create abundance from a place of lack. Just as you aligned the energy in your home to reflect your dreams, you can also cultivate an inner home that is a vibrational match to your desires.

Here is another example: I am so excited to move to a new house. The one I have right now just doesn't work. It is too small, it doesn't have enough light, and the ceilings are too low.

You can see how the focus is on what is not working versus an ideal vision for a new home—or the positive features in the current home that could be appreciated.

Any time you review something negative in the past, or complain about the present, or hear yourself say, "I want this but..." or "I would be happy if...," chances are you have split energy.

To realign with your desires, keep your attention on your intention (your heartfelt, clear desire) *and at the same time* look for things to love and appreciate about where you are now in this moment. I know this is easier said than done! Here are some tips to shift split energy and realign with your desires:

- Focus more on your goals. Read aloud your intentions and appreciate the physical affirmations you created.
- Put your attention on the positive aspects of the current situation, i.e., the things you do love about your house.
- Focus on what is working in your life, even if it is unrelated to your goal. For example, if your financial scene is not where you want it to be, but you have an amazing relationship, focus on the relationship.
- Focus on how you can feel good moment to moment—the little everyday things that bring you joy.

Unwavering Faith

The second inner key to manifesting is unwavering faith. To have unwavering faith is to know and feel wholeheartedly that your dreams will be realized. While unwavering faith is an ideal to strive towards, we can strengthen our faith by choosing new thoughts each time we find ourselves wavering.

Here are a few simple practices to cultivate faith:

- When you are making choices, ask yourself, how would I think, feel, and act if I trusted that the universe was infinitely abundant and looking out for my every need and answering my every desire?
- Make up a positive story: For example, if you are wondering why someone isn't calling you back, instead of imagining something negative, make up a positive story. For any such situation, ask yourself: How can I put a positive spin on this?
- Surround yourself with people who make you feel good and lift your energy and whose approach to life, values, and success you admire. As motivational speaker Jim Rohn says, "You are the average of the five people you spend the most time with." The more time you spend feeling good, the more you are a vibrational match for your desires. Relationships, along with your physical environment and your body, will have the greatest influence on your well-being and positivity.
- Look for examples that support an abundant view of the world and disprove limiting beliefs about lack. For example, if you have a limiting belief that you are too old to make a certain dream come true, or that it is too late or you are out of time, instead look for stories about people who transformed and succeeded later in life. This will force your brain to challenge your limiting belief. If it happened to someone else, you know it can happen to you!
- Look for the silver lining. Part of having unwavering faith is also trusting that everything is unfolding for your happiness and greater good, even when you face challenges or your goals are not realized. Sometimes, if a dream is not manifesting or things are not going your way, it is because the universe has even greater joy in store for you. You can trust that someday you will look back and realize there was a blessing in the detour or challenge.

Let Go: The 3rd Inner Key to Manifesting

When you are clear about your desires (key #1, maintain a clear positive focus) and you have faith that your dreams will be answered (key #2, unwavering faith), you are free to let go. Live life fully, be present, and look for things to appreciate each day. You do not need to keep checking in and wondering how it is going. Often, manifesting takes time and patience. Being overly focused and attached to your desires results in fear-based energy. Manifestations result from receiving and allowing, whereas holding on too tightly is the opposite energy. Relax, let go, and put your attention on the thoughts, people, things, and experiences that bring you joy each day.

Action Step: Align Your Inner Home?

Notice if you catch yourself "splitting your energy" and make note of it here. Next, choose from the list above to refocus your attention.

Any time we don't know why something is happening (or not happening) or someone is behaving in a certain way, we have a chance to spin a positive story. Is there a situation that is making you feel badly about yourself where you could write a positive story? Write the new story down here:

Pick a few of your limiting beliefs and write them down. Next to each belief write down proof of why the belief is not true. Even if you know one person or event that contradicts the belief, then you know it is not accurate.

Make a list of things in your life that bring you joy right now:

Week 46: Declutter Fear and Judgment

"Each day brings new opportunities to lean toward fear or lean toward love."

–Gabrielle Bernstein

Manifesting is an inner practice, with room for all of life's messiness and all our emotions. It is not about perfection or about always feeling good—it is about how quickly we can move back to awareness when we are off course and with, awareness, embrace and love all of who we are and all our emotions so that we can return to our natural state of allowing.

We have learned that the fastest way to return to center, to move through anxiety, depression, sadness or anger, is to move towards and into the feelings—to embrace and welcome them. Otherwise, "what you resist persists." We have also learned that it is not always helpful to get into our heads thinking about why we feel a certain way or what caused it. Rather we can drop into our bodies and simply feel and love the part of ourselves that is experiencing hurt.

We may also find ourselves worrying. Worrying is different from feeling our feelings. If you find yourself worrying about the future you will want to see first whether there is any action to be taken. Can you do anything about it? If not, then chances are you are stuck in fear and judgment. When we find ourselves in a negative thought pattern, or imagining and worrying about a negative future outcome, we have learned to follow a three-step process. This process has been so powerful for us that we call it the "secret to transformation in consciousness."

Here is a three-step process to use if you find yourself in fear, doubt, or worry (this process is similar to the four-step process for handling judgment as you declutter in Week 15):

1. Witness/Observe. Realize that any split energy or worry about events that haven't happened yet comes from fear, lack, limiting beliefs, and feelings of unworthiness. If you find yourself doubting that your dreams will manifest, engaging in negative self-talk, ruminating, or focusing on fearful what ifs—stop and observe the thoughts. If you find yourself feeling anxious or depressed, look for the thought behind the feeling. Next, observe by saying to yourself, "Oh, there is the fear" or "there is the self-judgment."

2. Forgive yourself for the judgment or thoughts. Underneath the fear based-thought is usually a judgment or belief. Say to yourself, "I forgive myself for buying into the belief that there is something wrong with me, that I have done something wrong, that I am left out and excluded from the good." Add any other belief you may have unearthed and forgive yourself for that belief.

3. Replace the thoughts, fear, or beliefs with a self-loving and compassionate statement, such as, "The truth is that I am human doing the best I can. The truth is that I am worthy, whole, and compete. The truth is that I am one with source energy." Next, turn your attention to your desires and affirm what you do want. "The truth is that my life is about joy, love, abundance, etc."

Action Step: Declutter Fear and Judgment

Each time you find yourself doubting your manifestations or caught in a worry loop, use the Three-Step Process. If you do this every time you catch the fear based thoughts, you will see a shift.

Week 47: Minimalist Affirmations: Themes and Mantras

"Whatever we plant in our subconscious mind and nourish with repetition and emotion will one day become a reality."
–Earl Nightingale

One great way to stay focused on your intentions and keep them fresh in your mind is to create what we call "Minimalist Affirmations." These affirmations are short phrases; emotionally charged, "juicy," personal words; or even the names of certain people that embody the quality you wish to integrate. When you *feel* what it is you desire—as opposed to just *thinking* it—you will embody the energy of your intention and be in a better place to recognize and experience the people and opportunities that will support your goals.

Minimalist affirmations will help you find the genuine feeling, positive energy, and true intention behind the affirmation. Sending a *feeling* intention out to the Universe is more powerful than saying words you do not quite believe.

How to Create a Minimalist Affirmation

1. Make it short. Instead of a detailed overthought sentence, make your affirmation brief. Two words are best, and they are often the first words that come to mind.

2. Choose positively charged and emotional words. This will be personal to you, but use heartfelt words that are fun to say. For example, instead of the prosperity affirmation "I am open and ready to receive wealth and prosperity in my life," use the minimalist affirmation "money magnet" (the double 'm' is fun to say, and money is a charged word, as is magnet, no pun intended).

3. Make it extreme, yet believable. Instead of creating an affirmation that would simply improve a situation, make one that captures the best possible outcome. For instance, if you are having a conflict with someone, rather than just affirming, "I am experiencing harmony in the relationship," take it to the extreme—every time you think of that person, you could say, "My hero-" which implies they are not only on your side, but advocating on your behalf.

4. Use words you do not typically use. Make it a little outside the box—a stretch even. Using words you do not normally use will allow you to truly hear the words rather than tune out and become numb to the meaning. But even though it is a stretch, it should still be crystal clear. When you say it, you should know exactly what you mean.

5. Fun is good. Making it a little quirky works because it brings a smile and lighthearted energy to the process. Typically, things manifest when we are less attached to outcomes and do not take things too seriously. A slightly humorous affirmation will lighten your energy.

Additional Ways to Use Minimalist Affirmations

1. Build minimalist affirmations into your to-do list. Minimalist affirmations will transform your to-do list from a chore into one giant affirmation. For example, replace the action step "learn how to use Excel" with "Excel master." Substitute "clear clutter and organize" with "tidy goddess."

2. Tap into someone else's consciousness. Pretend you are someone who has the quality or skill you desire. Think to yourself, "I am being so and so." For example, when I want to be a chill mom, I think, "Be Susan," because my friend Susan is always so calm. If I want to be the fun mom, I think, "Be Mary Poppins." The idea is that we are all one mind and one consciousness; therefore, you can "borrow" someone else's consciousness. In other words, if we are one, then if she has a quality in her, it is also within me.

3. Use your imagination and create a detailed, joyful fantasy. Daydream about a positive future fantasy. Make it a concrete vision; visualize where you are sitting, what you look like, who you are with, and how you are feeling. You could think about where you will be next New Year's Eve and imagine toasting all the wonderful things that happened that year.

4. Let the affirmation do the work. Sometimes a powerful affirmation is enough to create the energy we need to attract the positive outcome. Changing our language coupled with a genuine feeling behind the words will get the unconscious and right brain working, and things will line up with less effort.

5. Bring it into your everyday life. Particularly if you catch yourself doubting or having negative self-talk or thoughts—use the affirmations. Replace the negative thought with the affirmation. Almost like a mantra, sprinkle minimalist affirmations throughout your day.

Action Step: Make a Minimalist Affirmation

1. Revisit your life design: choose one of your intentions and create a minimalist affirmation for it. Write it down here:

____

____

____

____

____

2. Think of your affirmation like a mantra and say it to yourself several times a day, especially if you find yourself in fear or self-doubt.

Week 48: Caring for Your Inner Home

"Self-care is selfless service."
***–Dr. James Rouse,* Think, Eat, Move, Thrive**

You are now familiar with the idea that the key to manifesting is to think, feel, and behave in a way that is in alignment with your desires. Overall, the goal is to put yourself in the best state of being to access the possibilities available to you. By embracing inner practices, prioritizing self-care, and using your home to support inner practices and self-care habits, you will improve your well being and be in a better place to recognize, access, and take action when opportunity, insight, and inspiration present.

We feel most at home, happy, and content when both our inner and outer worlds are aligned. You have made changes in your home to positively influence your energy—working from the outside in. You have also made changes in your inner home and worked from the inside out. An internal shift contributes to the positive energy in your home. It is an inside-out and outside-in process: making space for love and creating a space that inspires love.

The best possible state of being to manifest easily is one of joy and appreciation. Below are some simple practices to cultivate inner peace, connection, gratitude, and joy throughout the day.

1. Morning intention. Before you get out of bed, set an intention for the day. It may be as simple as sending light to the day for the highest and greatest good, or simply asking that your day be filled with ease and grace.

2. Meditation. A daily meditation practice is a wonderful way to reduce stress and to focus within. Even if you don't have a meditation practice, you can "meditate" throughout your day by being mindful of the present moment, breathing deeply, or taking time to sit quietly.

3. Commune with nature. Nature inspires a sense of calm and reduces stress. Go for a walk or hike or if you have a backyard, patio, or balcony, spend time outside. Spending time outside early in the day supports sleep at night. You can also bring nature indoors by bringing plants, fresh flowers, bowls of fruit, or potted herbs into your home. Pulling back curtains and opening blinds and windows to let in fresh air and sunlight also connects us to nature and lifts our spirits.

4. Gratitude. Gratitude instantly shifts our perspective and moves us out of fear and into a heart-centered space. In challenging times, it is easy to be grateful for things we may have taken for granted, such as good health, family, and the love, freedom, and peace in our lives. Studies have shown that gratitude reduces stress and increases happiness. Before you fall asleep is a great time to think of things you are grateful for. You may even write them down in a journal.

5. Listen more and speak kindly. In his book The Four Agreements, Don Miguel Ruiz' suggests "saying only what is true, kind and necessary."

6. Practice mindfulness as you care for your home. Every moment is an opportunity to practice intentional living (purpose) and consciousness (awareness)—even our daily acts of home-keeping, such as sorting through the mail, cooking, cleaning, and tidying. Coming from a place of acceptance and appreciation as you care for your home (versus judgment and lack) will strengthen your inner home and simultaneously enhance your physical surroundings. Tuning your focus to the moment and connecting within throughout the day will carry you from one present (moment) to the next present (moment).

7. Eat mindfully. Take a moment to give thanks for food or ask that the food be filled with a healthy, loving energy. Eat mindfully and slowly, focusing on the tastes, textures, colors, and beauty of your food.

8. Ask for assistance. We have come to learn that one of the most powerful practices is asking for help. In addition to asking for help from professionals, family, and friends, we make a habit of asking for Spirit's assistance. (We use the word "Spirit" to mean source energy—the life force and intelligence that connects everything. Of course, for you it may be God, your higher self, the universe, mother earth, etc.) In our experience, when we ask for assistance, it is given in one form or another. It is comforting to know that we always have support.

9. Breathing. Take slow deep breaths throughout the day.

10. Silence. It is easy to fill our minds and days from when we wake up until we go to bed. Usually, most of our doings are pre-planned. The problem with this is that we need space and silence to create an opening for inspiration, for guidance, and for something new to happen. The silence gives space for the universe to provide in extraordinary ways that we could not have imagined.

11. Drink water throughout the day. In addition to being essential to our survival, spiritually water is often used as a blessing and is associated with cleansing and well-being.

12. Take a break. Taking breaks throughout the day is an act of self love. What refreshes you? Teatime, lying on the floor and breathing, a walk, or maybe a catnap?

13. Embrace a mantra, quote, or saying. Examples: Spirit provides ; Life is good; This is happening for me, not to me; Peace, be still; The only time is Now; Thank you, God, for everything.

14. Choose Love. In *Conversations with God*, Neale Donald Walsch encourages us to ask in each moment, "What would love do now?" We suppose this really sums it up!

Action Step: Adopt a Simple Inner Practice or Self-Care Habit

Which simple practices would you like to incorporate into your day?

____

____

____

____

Which self-care habit do you wish to support?

How can your home support this practice and habit? What can you add, reposition, or remove in your home to inspire and support consistent action?

Week 49: Inspired Everyday Living

"Joy comes to us in ordinary moments. We risk missing out on joy when we get too busy chasing down the extraordinary."

-Brené Brown

Our attention is often drawn to the big events—the birthday celebrations, graduations, promotions, and the like—but in fact, it is the little everyday moments—making meals, helping with homework, walking the dog, paying the bills, getting dressed—that account for most of our life. And the majority of these everyday moments take place in our homes.

This is why creating a home we love—a place that is clutter-free and organized and that supports our goals and reflects our dreams—is essential. When we are empowered and inspired by our homes, we can show up for these everyday moments at our best—present and connected. How we are in each of these mundane moments ... is life. Ideally, the hours spent preparing for the birthday party are just as special as the event itself. Life is now.

Rhythm and Ritual

We believe that a simplified environment + rhythm and ritual = inspired everyday living. Everyday routines and daily, weekly, or seasonal rituals ground us and connect us. Knowing what comes next is comforting and freeing. The more everyone in the home knows what to expect and has their routines and responsibilities in place, the more everyone can enjoy the moment. There is freedom in form! Rituals offer something to look forward to and quality time for connection. Here are some examples of routines and rituals: making beds and tidying up in the morning, journaling, sit-down family meals, movie nights, weekly meal planning and menus, bedtime rituals, afternoon tea break, game nights, afternoon walks, reading before bed.

A clutter-free and intentional home allows us to be present for ourselves and our loved ones during these everyday moments. This presence is what gives rise to inspired everyday living

Action Step: Support Rhythm and Rituals

Do you have daily/weekly/monthly routines and rituals that have you already established?

Daily:

Weekly:

Monthly:

Can you think of any you would like to add to your days, weeks, or months or let go of?

Add:

Let go of?

Are there any parts of your days or weeks that you find challenging (getting out the door in the morning, meal times, etc.)?

What changes could you make in your home to support a smooth routine?

You could also consider an inner shift such as practicing mindfulness and gratitude. What might prompt you to adopt this new perspective?

If you identified a change you could make in your home to support everyday living, make that change.

If you identify a new ritual or routine you would like to embrace, add it to your calendar until it becomes a habit.

Week 50: Appreciation

"Whatever you are grateful for multiplies. Gratitude is the great multiplier."

***–Rhonda Byrne,* The Power**

"Be grateful for the home you have, knowing that at this moment, all you have is all you need."

–Sarah Ban Breathnach

It is easy to get distracted by home improvement projects, clutter, or images of picture-perfect homes, but this only leads to focusing on what isn't working in your home. We have clients who have admitted to not cooking in the kitchen for fear of messing it up, or clients who lament that they can't enjoy their children's play without thinking about picking up the toys. The point of clearing clutter is to live fully and freely expressed in the present moment and thoroughly enjoy our homes. If you find yourself being a perfectionist, as I myself often do, the way out is through appreciation.

We can not underemphasize the importance of gratitude and appreciation when it comes to creating a life we love. Focusing on and appreciating what is working in our lives puts us in the best possible place to recognize and access the opportunities, experiences, information, and people that will be essential on the path to our dreams.

Through appreciation we can cultivate contentment and be at peace with our homes.

Action Step: Appreciation Exercises

Exercise 1

The moment you wake up, look for things you appreciate about your home. Continue this exercise throughout your day. Do you love your soft sheets, the way the light shines through your window in the morning, or the color of your walls? Whatever you find, take a moment to appreciate the usefulness, beauty, or good feelings it inspires.

Exercise 2

1. Find a comfy place to sit in your home with pen and paper. Close your eyes and take a few deep breaths. When you open your eyes, look around your home. Make a list of all the things you appreciate and why.

2. Give thanks for everything on the list.

Exercise 3

In whatever way feels true for you, start communicating with your home. This could be as simple as pulling back curtains and opening windows with a grateful heart in the mornings, saying good night to your home as you turn off the lights in the evenings, or saying thank you when you feel grateful.

Week 51: Celebrate

"Lasting happiness starts with one question...what can I celebrate?"

- Michael B. Beckwith

"The more you praise and celebrate your life, the more there is in life to celebrate."

- Oprah Winfrey

Cultivating a feeling of celebration—both by living as if your dreams were already manifest and by celebrating where you are now and how far you have come—is an inner practice that will support your manifestations.

Celebrating our personal wins—including our small accomplishments—boosts our motivation, increasing the likelihood that we will realize our larger goals. Our brains love completion and rewards; when we complete a task or celebrate a win, dopamine levels increase and this creates a positive feedback loop that propels you to keep going.*

Also, celebrating feels good—when we acknowledge our success we naturally feel grateful and uplifted! Celebrations cause us to appreciate and honor who we already are—and what we already have—as opposed to putting attention on the things we don't have or our shortcomings. This mindset is key to manifesting because, as we have been explaining, manifestation is truly a process of revealing; the things we desire already exist and we are in essence unlimited potential—to manifest we are simply aligning, creating space, and allowing so that our desires are made visible.

Celebrate who you already are!

*https://hbr.org/2016/03/your-desire-to-get-things-done-can-undermine-your-effectiveness

What do you appreciate about yourself?

List your recent accomplishments and manifestations: remember these can be small wins, tasks you completed, progress towards your goals, sticking with a new habit, serving someone else, such as your community, friend, or family member, or inner work—i.e. loving myself as I decluttered by refraining from judgment.

One of the best ways to cultivate a celebratory way of living life at home is to elevate everyday moments into a celebration. Here are 10 ideas to elevate everyday living into a celebration:

1. Find ways to turn the ordinary into extraordinary, such as transforming a family dinner into a dinner party—mostly by simply calling it a dinner party and perhaps by adding candles, flowers, and a special treat.
2. Create your own mini-holidays by adding celebratory rituals to your week—such as a Friday movie night or Tuesday tacos.
3. Stay present as you cook, wash dishes, and clean. Make this time rewarding by playing music, listening to a favorite podcast, or using cleaning products with a great scent.
4. Treat yourself well now—use the best dishes and napkins everyday.
5. Light candles for your bath and your children's bath.
6. Take a walk after dinner.
7. Turn on music and dance.
8. Keep fresh flowers in your home all the time, not just when you expect company.
9. Go to bed early with your favorite book or stack of magazines.
10. Allow yourself to do absolutely nothing—to let go of efficiency and to-do lists and time. Follow your heart.

Action Step: Celebrate

1. Make celebrating yourself and your wins a practice: Consider adding your wins and accomplishments to your daily gratitude list.

2. Use the best of everything now. Don't wait to use your best dishes or cloth

napkins, light the expensive candle, or wear your best outfit. When we put things on hold for "someday," we send ourselves the message that it's okay to delay our dreams, or that we are not whole and worthy in this moment, or that our dream life and happiness is dependent upon external circumstances.

3. How might you celebrate this week, or in the coming weeks? Choose from the list above, or imagine your own celebration:

Week 52: Contribution

"One person can make a difference. Instilling an oasis of peace into your home, in a small corner of the universe, can make all the difference in the world."
***–Denise Linn,* Sacred Space**

As our dreams come to fruition and we cultivate the spirit of celebration, there is a natural tendency to contribute by sharing our gifts or helping others create their own ideal homes and lives. This contribution could be as simple as sharing a resource or your own experience.

We encourage you to take your successes and your feeling of being at home out into the world!

Peaceful Home, Peaceful Life, Peaceful World

Everything is connected. I believe that the happiness, health, and peace you create in your own home and in yourself makes a difference—not only in your own life, but in others' as well.

When you live in a peaceful space, when you make a nurturing home, when you create the dwelling of your dreams, you take this energy with you. You bring this feeling of home out into the world, where you will serve and uplift others.

You may contribute through kindness and choosing love in each moment or looking for things to appreciate about everyone and every situation.

There are also practical ways you can contribute: by sharing what you have learned with others, donating mindfully, or caring for your larger home, mother earth.

Action Step: Contribute

How do you envision yourself contributing? What calls to you and inspires you?

Is there someone you have been thinking of reaching out to or something you have thought about doing?

If something comes to mind, what would be the next step? (Remember to make your next step easy and doable, so that you are excited to take action.)

Reflect on your wins and successes. How have your manifestations served you and contributed to those around you? (Remember that even the seemingly small changes count, such as shifting your nighttime routine and making some changes in your bedroom leading to better sleep, which serves your health and well-being, which then contributes to your family because you are more calm and loving.)

If you are not clear as to how you can contribute you could put it out to the universe with the question "How may I serve ?" and see what transpires.

Let's Be in Touch

You did it! Congratulations on completing the 52 weeks! It is my greatest wish that you have created space in your home and moved yourself closer to your highest, most heartfelt vision for yourself and your life. I imagine you living your dream at home and am excited to hear about the manifestations that unfold.

Keep in mind that everything is evolving. As you grow and change (even throughout this process), so too must your environment. Continue to check-in with your home and the items within it and revisit this journal! Reflect on where you have been, examine where you are now, and keep setting intentions for where you would like to go. Your home's purpose is to serve you—with just a little intention and action, it will meet you wherever you are in each moment.

Please also know that Alison and I are still here for you. We would love to welcome you into our online community where we can continue to support you and hear about your wins. Here are the ways to connect with us, as well as some additional FREE resources:

- Join our community for weekly tips and inspiration delivered to your inbox at inspiredeverydayliving.com/blog

- Take our free recorded Decluttering class: inspiredeverydayliving.com

- Learn about our courses and one-on-one consultations: inspiredeverydayliving.com/work-with-us

- Follow us on Instagram @inspired.everyday.living

With gratitude,
Laura and Alison

Appendix I: Room-by-Room Obvious Clutter

Kitchen

- Excess paper and plastic bags: Recycle the plastic and paper bags. Invest in sturdy, washable, reusable grocery totes, so you can avoid accumulating this type of clutter.
- Excess rubber bands and twist ties: At some point we all end up with more than we will ever need! Sometimes these items can be useful for a local preschool.
- Excess dish towels: Just keep the ones you use and that fit nicely in the space you have.
- Expired food and pantry items: After disposing of the food, recycle any jars or cans to avoid the next type of clutter on this list.
- Excess Tupperware, glass jars, and other food storage containers (especially those with missing lids).
- Take out menus: You can always locate the menu online.
- Duplicates or different sizes of the same of kitchen utensils and gadgets: Keep only the ones you use. If an item serves the same purpose, choose the size or type that you like the best and let go of the rest.
- Excess disposables (chopsticks, cutlery etc.): It is easy to accumulate these items especially if you order out a lot. When you place a to go order you can often specify whether or not you need eating utensils to avoid this type of clutter.
- Cookbooks: Unless you love the cookbook—maybe it is sentimental or beautiful—it is easier, space saving, and more accessible to copy your favorite recipes and put them all in one binder or digital folder.

Bathroom

- Expired prescriptions and over-the-counter medicines.
- Old makeup and skincare items, including sunblock: Check the expiration date.
- Empty shampoo, lotion, toothpaste, and other bottles: Recycle these to keep your space tidy.
- Free samples and hotel shampoo, soap, lotion etc. Only keep a few that you know you will use. Or if you have a guest room, keep two sets.
- Excess or stretched-out hair ties.
- Old or dried-out nail polish.
- Excess towels. If you do laundry often, usually one set is enough. And two sets is plenty. For those who keep an old towel for muddy messes, usually one is enough.

Laundry Room or Closet

- Excess linens: We find it is best to have 1 to 2 sets maximum of linens per bed. We wash our bed linens and then put them right back on the bed. This way, you save on storage space and never have to fold! We do the same with bath towels as well.
- Stained or torn towels or linens: Save a few for rags and donate or recycle the rest. Sometimes animal shelters have a need for towels and linens.
- Excess rags: Just keep what you use.
- Cleaning products samples: let go of any you never intend to use.
- Excess laundry baskets.
- Broken appliances or duplicates.

Bedroom

- Excess books you don't plan to read: A backlog of books stacked on a bedside table can feel overwhelming.
- Hanger from the drycleaners: Unwrap any dry cleaning and return the hangers for a calmer, more cohesive closet.
- Shopping bags and shoe boxes: Unless you use these for storage your closet will feel tidier without these items.

Items that don't belong in the bedroom: Anything that does not promote sleep and intimacy is best stored in a different location.

Living Room

- Outdated magazines: Unless they are sentimental or you reference them frequently, chances are you can do without (and always find a backcopy online if need be).
- VHS tapes and DVDs (unless of course you still watch them).

Office

- Unused supplies: Recycle excess paper, rubber bands, paperclips, etc.
- Duplicate supplies: Usually one stapler, scissors, etc. suffices.
- Outdated and unused electronics: CDs, VHS, keyboards, mouse, cords, adaptors etc., especially those that don't work with your current devices.
- Paper clutter: Receipts, notes, old files, documents. Any paper that you do not need to save can be recycled. You can also create a digital system by scanning documents to save storage space and cut down on visual clutter.

Children's Items

- Art and school supplies: Dried up markers, glue, and excess art and school supplies. Choose a set of markers and crayons. Half-used notebooks don't often get used; recycle any excess paper.
- Party favors, freebies, and swag.
- Outgrown toys and clothes: Donate or save for a sibling the ones that are in good repair, and let go of the rest.

Other

- User Manuals: You can save space and find these online
- Spare change: Designate one container in the home for spare change.

Appendix 2: Room-by-Room Clutter-Clearing Plan

Bedrooms

often associated with self-care & romance

- ❑ Bedside Tables
- ❑ Dresser Tops, Bookshelves, or Mantles
- ❑ Storage Under the Bed
- ❑ Armoire
- ❑ ____________________
- ❑ ____________________

Clothes Closet

often associated with self-care and self-empowerment

- ❑ T-shirts and tanks
- ❑ Blouses/shirts
- ❑ Sweaters
- ❑ Pants/Shorts
- ❑ Dresses/Skirts/Suits
- ❑ Jackets & Coats (if your coats are spread out among other parts of your home, such as a coat closet or front entry, bring all your coats together when you clear)
- ❑ Workout Clothes and Swimwear
- ❑ Undergarments
- ❑ Socks

- ❑ Shoes
- ❑ Jewelry and/or Ties
- ❑ Hats, Scarves, Gloves
- ❑ Bags and Purses
- ❑ ____________________
- ❑ ____________________

Bathrooms

often associated with health and self-care

- ❑ Medicine Cabinet
- ❑ Make-up/Bathroom Drawers
- ❑ Shower/Tub
- ❑ Under the sink
- ❑ ____________________
- ❑ ____________________

Kitchens

often associated with health and family

- ❑ Counters
- ❑ Kitchen Table
- ❑ Drawers & Cabinets (you may wish to divide this into smaller areas by working on one category at a time)
- ❑ Pots & Pans
- ❑ Bowls & Baking
- ❑ Cooking Utensils
- ❑ Baking Utensils
- ❑ Appliances
- ❑ Food-storage Containers (recycle any that do not have matching tops)
- ❑ Dishes
- ❑ Glassware
- ❑ Silverware
- ❑ Table Linens
- ❑ Spices

- ❑ Food/Pantry
- ❑ Junk Drawer
- ❑ Cleaning Supplies
- ❑ ______________________
- ❑ ______________________

Living Rooms

often associated with friends and family

- ❑ Bookshelves
- ❑ Media Console
- ❑ Coffee Tables
- ❑ Mantles
- ❑ ______________________
- ❑ ______________________

Kids Bedrooms and Play Spaces

often associated with family and creativity

- ❑ Toy Bins
- ❑ Bookshelves
- ❑ Children's Clothes Closet/ Dresser
- ❑ ______________________
- ❑ ______________________

Garages and Storage

often associated with the subconscious

- ❑ Tool Chest
- ❑ Yard or Gardening Equipment
- ❑ Sports Equipment Storage
- ❑ Holiday Decoration Storage
- ❑ Miscellaneous Storage
- ❑ ______________________
- ❑ ______________________

Entryways

often associated with new opportunities

- ❑ Consoles
- ❑ Closet
- ❑ Drawers
- ❑ ______________________
- ❑ ______________________

Mudrooms & Laundry Rooms

often associated with self-care and family

- ❑ Cabinets
- ❑ Cleaning Supplies
- ❑ Miscellaneous or "Junk" Drawers
- ❑ Cubbies
- ❑ ______________________
- ❑ ______________________

Home Office or Desk

often associated with career and wealth

- ❑ Desktop
- ❑ Papers
- ❑ Office Supplies
- ❑ Drawers
- ❑ Files
- ❑ Computer's digital clutter
- ❑ ______________________
- ❑ ______________________

Acknowledgements

I feel like the luckiest person in the world when it comes to attracting talented, brilliant, conscious, wise, and loving support. This book was no exception. It would not have been possible without those who follow. I am so grateful for you all:

First and foremost my sister, Alison Forbes Van Hook, for her partnership in business and for being the best sister anyone could ever ask for in life, and of course for her brilliant contributions to this book.

My teachers, whose wisdom and spirits are true gifts: Rev. Cheryl Ward; Rev. Michael Beckwith; Drs. Ron and Mary Hulnick; Gay Hendricks, Ph.D.; Dr. Sue Morter; Terah Kathryn Collins; Sandra Eagle; and Kit Wilkins.

My editor, Shawn Mihalik, for his guidance and skillful touch.

My coach, Martha Bullen, for her patience, persistence, and process that ushered me through the publishing process.

Maggie McLaughlin for helping me navigate KDP.

Abby Weintraub for her generosity and beautiful cover design.

My friends, who are always with me whether we are together or not.

My Dad for his insights and encouragement.

My mom for her unending care and love.

My sons, James and Matthew—who are the greatest blessings in my life.

My husband, Scott, for his unconditional love and support—and always seeing the best in me.

Our Inspired Everyday Living Community for sharing your homes, lives, and wisdom. You inspire us ... every day! Thank You.

About the Author

Laura Forbes Carlin, along with her sister Alison Forbes Van Hook, is the cofounder of Inspired Everyday Living, an online resource for creating a life you love through the process of creating a home you love. She is the coauthor of *Decluttering for Parents* and the co-creator of the online course *Declutter and Manifest*. Her passion for decluttering and organizing began when she was nine years old.

For the past twenty years, she has been providing tips, inspiration, and step-by-step guidance to her community on how to make simple changes in their homes to create positive changes in their lives. She has appeared in *The Washington Post*, *The Today Show*, KTLA, *Goop*, *Traditional Home*, *C Magazine*, and *The Hollywood Reporter*.

Laura holds an MA in Spiritual Psychology and a BS in communications from Northwestern University, and she is a Simplicity Parenting Coach™. She lives with her husband and their two sons in Los Angeles and Sun Valley, Idaho.

To learn more or contact Laura, visit www.inspiredeverydayliving.com.

Printed in Great Britain
by Amazon

53981555R00117